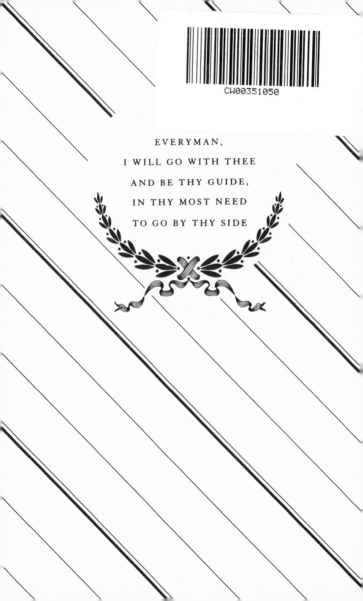

EVERYMAN,
I WILL GO WITH THEE
AND BE THY GUIDE,
IN THY MOST NEED
TO GO BY THY SIDE

EVERYMAN'S LIBRARY
POCKET POETS

PICTURE-HOUSE POEMS

••••••••••••••••••••

EDITED BY
HAROLD SCHECHTER
AND MICHAEL WATERS

EVERYMAN'S LIBRARY
POCKET POETS

Alfred A. Knopf New York London Toronto

THIS IS A BORZOI BOOK
PUBLISHED BY ALFRED A. KNOPF

This selection by Harold Schechter and Michael Waters first published in
Everyman's Library, 2019

www.randomhouse/everymans
www.everymanslibrary.co.uk

ISBN: 978-1-101-90803-7 (US)
978-1-84159-814-7 (UK)

A CIP catalogue reference for this book is available from the
British Library

Typography by Peter B. Willberg

Typeset in the UK by Input Data Services Ltd, Isle Abbotts, Somerset

Printed and bound in Germany by GGP Media GmbH, Pössneck

CONTENTS

5

6

REMAKES

REEL LIFE

FOREWORD

If, as Henry David Thoreau says, "our truest lives are when we are in dreams awake," then millions of people have led, if not their truest, certainly their most vivid lives in darkened theaters, immersed in the trans-porting dreams unreeling before their open eyes. The narrator of Walker Percy's classic novel, *The Moviegoer*, speaks for many in recalling the high points of his life: "Other people, so I have read, treasure memorable moments in their lives: the time one climbed the Pan-theon at sunrise, the summer night one met a lonely girl in Central Park and achieved with her a sweet and natural relationship, as they say in books. I, too, once met a girl in Central Park, but it is not much to remem-ber. What I remember is the time John Wayne killed three men with a carbine as he was falling to the dusty street in *Stagecoach*. And the time the kitten found Orson Welles in the doorway in *The Third Man*."

That poets – practitioners of what is traditionally viewed as the most rarefied of arts – should devote their writings to a medium as demotic as the movies might seem paradoxical at a glance. But as the poet Vachel Lindsay was the first to acknowledge, the deities of the ancient pantheon have been replaced in the modern world by the gods and goddesses of the silver screen. Far from being mere entertainment, the movies constitute the myths of our time. In the century since the birth of the Hollywood studios, poets, as the works collected here attest, have been deeply engaged with the movies, exploring the countless ways those celluloid dreams have nourished, excited, and shaped the modern imagination.

Harold Schechter
Michael Waters

POPCORN PALACES

SOUTH INDIAN CINEMA

Green girls stomp in their saris,
Elephants with warrior-princes
Pinned to howdahs sway in the middle distance,
A villain with his waxed mustache
A hero with plump rouged face
Chase each other round the temple tank.
A bird, a real bird in a mango tree
Utterly unplanned, drops its offerings onto a baby's
      head,
He gurgles in delight while our heroine
In satin sari and backless blouse
Starts her wild untutored weeping for the cameraman.
So time passes in Tirunalveli or Tiruchirapalli –
Half a mile away in Love Good Ciné Hall
At Interval time, just after the sale of Limca and
      Tuttifruitti
And tiny pakoras fried to a crisp
A boy half naked leaps into the stalls
And waves his arms in delight, signaling the gods.
Cigarettes drop from his khaki shorts
Some of them are half burnt tips he has gathered
To share with his unborn brother,
Some flutter into apsara wings.

MEENA ALEXANDER (1951–)   15

LOEW'S TRIBORO

It was easy as lying to our mothers. As living in
    Queens
  across from Manhattan, walking over
the bridge connecting three boroughs, looking
down on the nut house on Ward's Island, one of us
    dribbling a basketball. Eggs in our

pockets, we sneaked into the Loew's theater through
    the back door. The old vaudeville stage
behind the movie screen moving with the shadow of
Bogart and his lisp. One of us just out of jail for
    sticking
  up a drugstore. His father leaving him

there two extra days to teach him a lesson. We
    climbed
  up the ladder along the side of the
screen, behind a fake Renaissance curtain, looked
    out at
the audience in the dark, the glowing cigarettes, Hank,
    whose father ran a dry-goods store

on Steinway Street, slipping his hand under a girl's
     skirt.
  Checking the material. A script
flickering at our loins. The newsreel releasing
     survivors
into sunlight, arms thin as the stripes on their
     pajamas.
  Eleanor's father on the corner of Broadway

waving pamphlets for the Labor Party. Eleanor
     not yet
  in her marine boyfriend's room getting
shot to death. We reached the little balcony, the
     Wurlitzer
organ draped with an old carpet, the bad smell of
     Father
  Flaherty's breath. We kept going.

At the top of the screen, from behind a decorative
     molding, we saw our neighbors sucking
Black Crows, rolling darkness in their mouths. And
we started. The eggs cool from Sonny's aunt's
     refrigerator flew across

the night sky blinking down from light-bulb space.
        They
    landed like doves breaking apart on Hank's
chest, a gooey wound on the girl's skirt. They slid out
        of our
hands like ghosts, uncle's loud jokes descending at his
    sister's second wedding, groans

splurting in the night, a rifled mischief rotating in
        the air,
    concussed, spun by history's grooves,
while Jerry down there with his polio leg in a brace
raised himself on the splattered yolky arms of his seat
    and roared, shaking his fist.

DOUBLE FEATURE

At Dunbar, Castle or Arcade
we rode with the exotic sheik
through deserts of erotic flowers;
held in the siren madonna's arms
were safe from the bill-collector's power.

Forgave the rats and roaches we
could not defeat, beguiled by jazzbo
strutting of a mouse. And when
the Swell Guy, roused to noblest wrath
shot down all those weakéd men,

Oh how we cheered to see the good we were
destroy the bad we'd never be.
What mattered then the false, the true
at Dunbar, Castle or Arcade,
where we were other for an hour or two?

ROBERT HAYDEN (1913–80)   19

1948: SATURDAYS

Every Saturday morning
before my father left to open the store
he'd leave a dollar on the dresser so
Susie and I could go to the movies

Every Saturday:
The Loews Gates or the RKO Bushwick

With that dollar we could get two 25 cent tickets
and have plenty left over for Raisinets (her) and
Goobers (me) plus popcorn, but
we had to sit in the children's section
a noisy little ghetto ruled by The Matron
a large woman in a white uniform, with a big
    flashlight
and a terrible temper, no wonder. I think the same
    woman
managed to be present simultaneously in every theater
    in Brooklyn
We'd sit through the double feature and the cartoons,
    the coming
attractions and "the chapter," at least once, maybe
    twice,
Then, to really get our money's worth,
make noise and throw stuff until we got thrown out

When I turned 12, I had to pay the adult admission:
    50 cents
but – I still bristle at the injustice – the law said you
    had to
sit in the children's section until you were 16.
    Imagine.
Sometimes we'd show up and the children's section
    was full!
You could only get in if you were accompanied by an
    adult
One of us, let's say me, would linger near the box
    office until some poor
dope with a hangover would show up at noon. Hey
    mister, hey mister
take me in with you? Yeah, okay (mumbled). And my
    friends, too, mister?
(They emerged from the shadows.) Please, my friends
    too?
Okay, okay. It was only after we were inside that
the poor bastard learned his horrible fate. These kids
    come in with you?
(Dull nod) Then they got to sit with you!

When I turned 14, large enough to pass for 16, I made
    my break. I got
to escape to the balcony. To sit by myself in the
    balcony, in the embracing dark
by myself, smoking Lucky Strikes. By myself high up
    in the dark.
It was the beginning of what I thought of as
    adulthood and
I thought it would just keep getting better and better

THE SKOKIE THEATRE

Twelve years old and lovesick, bumbling
and terrified for the first time in my life,
but strangely hopeful, too, and stunned,
definitely stunned – I wanted to cry,
I almost started to sob when Chris Klein
actually touched me – oh God – below the belt
in the back row of the Skokie Theatre.
Our knees bumped helplessly, our mouths
were glued together like flypaper, our lips
were grinding in a hysterical grimace
while the most handsome man in the world
twitched his hips on the flickering screen
and the girls began to scream in the dark.
I didn't know one thing about the body yet,
about the deep foam filling my bones,
but I wanted to cry out in desolation
when she touched me again, when the lights
flooded on in the crowded theatre
and the other kids started to file
into the narrow aisles, into a lobby
of faded purple splendor, into the last
Saturday in August before she moved away.
I never wanted to move again, but suddenly
we were being lifted toward the sidewalk
in a crush of bodies, blinking, shy,

unprepared for the ringing familiar voices
and the harsh glare of sunlight, the brightness
of an afternoon that left us gripping
each other's hands, trembling and changed.

MOVIES

The Roosevelt, Renaissance, Gem, Alhambra:
Harlem laughing in all the wrong places
   at the crocodile tears
   of crocodile art
   that you know
   in your heart
   is crocodile:

      (Hollywood
      laughs at me,
      black –
      so I laugh
      back.)

LANGSTON HUGHES (1902–67)   25

POEM ENDING IN ANTARCTICA

The darkness of a theater I hate it
though I think of you when I'm there
let me be honest I hate cinema
all aspects of it   an unpopular notion
and this is a love poem that begins
with us watching *Killer of Sheep*
because you love film and I wanted
to exercise the greatest pleasure
the French guy says about the movies
which is leaving
with you on my arm   see?
Isn't this better than that dancing
cone of light of which
you'd later write so beautifully
and I'm stealing because theft
is more intimate than respect?
Exit sign metal push doors
sky the everywhere–Drano smell
then the tyranny of what I must take in
leaches away with every step
I feel purer baptized even
whenever I'm done with a film
and I can jump out of my chewing-
gum seat but this happens
whether you are with me or not

and for a time you weren't
which is why I could think of you
in that darkness when I was sitting
in the grime of so many fantasies
enacted in one dark room   mine too
bumping and elbowing their way
through the crowd until they appeared
in the shape of a girl
about to lose her organs I'm not kidding
they take them away one by one
until she drops dead   my decay
the last ten years of good health
spent without you when the next ten
could be all biopsies and copays
and why was our last movie
Killer of Sheep   so terribly sad
when we could have laughed through
Encounters at the End of the World
where eighty kilometers from shore
on a plain of ice Herzog asks a scientist
if in the interior of that vast continent
there's such a thing as going plain crazy
realizing one's damned had enough
and yes the answer is always absolutely yes

ESTHER LIN (1982–)   27

AVE MARIA

Mothers of America
        let your kids go to the movies!
get them out of the house so they won't know what
      you're up to
it's true that fresh air is good for the body
                        but what about the soul
that grows in darkness, embossed by silvery images
and when you grow old as grow old you must
                        they won't hate you
they won't criticize you they won't know
        they'll be in some glamorous country
they first saw on a Saturday afternoon or playing
      hookey

they may even be grateful to you
                   for their first sexual experience
which only cost you a quarter
                and didn't upset the peaceful home
they will know where candy bars come from
               and gratuitous bags of popcorn
as gratuitous as leaving the movie before it's over
with a pleasant stranger whose apartment is in the
                   Heaven on Earth Bldg
near the Williamsburg Bridge
        oh mothers you will have made the little tykes

so happy because if nobody does pick them up in the
     movies
they won't know the difference
                    and if somebody does it'll be sheer gravy
and they'll have been truly entertained either way
instead of hanging around the yard
                         or up in their room
                                   hating you

prematurely since you won't have done anything
     horribly
                                   mean yet
except keeping them from the darker joys
                         it's unforgivable the latter
so don't blame me if you won't take this advice
                         and the family breaks up
and your children grow old and blind in front of a
     TV set
                                   seeing
movies you wouldn't let them see when they were
     young

FRANK O'HARA (1929–66)   29

DOUBLE FEATURE

With Buck still tied to the log, on comes the light.
Lovers disengage, move sheepishly toward the aisle
With mothers, sleep-heavy children, stale perfume,
       past
    the manager's smile
Out through the velvety chains to the cool air of night.

I dawdle with groups near the rickety pop-corn stand;
Dally at shop windows, still reluctant to go;
I teeter, heels hooked on the curb, scrape a toe;
Or send off a car with vague lifts of a hand.

A wave of Time hangs motionless on this particular
       shore.
I notice a tree, arsenical grey in the light, or the slow
Wheel of the stars, the Great Bear glittering colder
       than snow,
And remember there was something else I was
       hoping for.

CONCESSIONS

The more it costs the less it's worth
so nothing's sweeter than three percent

of the nine hundred percent profit
a small soda pours syrupy into the scales

of commerce. Kernels of gold and oil
too yellow with coconut tropical dreams

copper the air with the irresistible
breeze of heat and salt like water

priming the pump for thirst, the call
for sweet in special-sized boxes larger

than a needy tongue's coffin. Stretch
the plastic liquid cheese with the briny

residue of metallic jalapeños until
the boats of chips drown with only

the green rings preserving whatever
remnant of life flavor had. And rolling,

forever rolling like fat logs from
a child's forgotten cabin disassembled

on the grill, the sweating franks wait
for the soft doughy loads to tuck in,

blanketed in yellow or red or both and
nestle in the dark. *Let's all go to the lobby* . . .

MOVIE HOUSE

View it, by day, from the back,
from the parking lot in the rear,
for from this angle only
the beautiful brick blankness can be grasped.
Monumentality
wears one face in all ages.

No windows intrude real light
into this temple of shades,
and the size of it,
the size of the great rear wall measures
the breadth of the dreams we have had here.

It dwarfs the village bank,
outlooms the town hall,
and even in its decline
makes the bright-ceilinged supermarket seem mean.

Stark closet of stealthy rapture,
vast introspective camera
wherein our most daring self-projections
were given familiar names:
stand, stand by your macadam lake

and tell the aeons of our extinction
that we too could house our gods,
could secrete a pyramid
to sight the stars by.

AT THE MOVIE: VIRGINIA, 1956

This is how it was:
they had their own churches, their own schools,
schoolbuses, football teams, bands and majorettes,
separate restaurants, in all the public places
their own bathrooms, at the doctor's
their own waiting room, in the *Tribune*
a column for their news, in the village
a neighborhood called Sugar Hill,
uneven rows of unresponsive houses
that took the maids back in each afternoon –
in our homes used the designated door,
on Trailways sat in the back, and at the movie
paid at a separate entrance, stayed upstairs.
Saturdays, a double feature drew the local kids
as the town bulged, families surfacing
for groceries, medicine and wine,
the black barber, white clerks in the stores – crowds
lined the sidewalks, swirled through the courthouse
    yard,
around the stone soldier and the flag,

and still I never *saw* them on the street.
It seemed a chivalric code
laced the milk: you'd try not to look
and they would try to be invisible.

Once, on my way to the creek,
I went without permission to the tenants'
log cabin near the barns, and when Aunt Susie
opened the door, a cave yawned, and beyond her
        square,
leonine, freckled face, in the hushed interior,
Joe White lumbered up from the table, six unfolding
feet of him, dark as a gun-barrel, his head bent
to clear the chinked rafters, and I caught
the terrifying smell of sweat and grease,
smell of the woodstove, nightjar, straw mattress –

This was rural Piedmont, upper south;
we lived on a farm but not in poverty.
When finally we got our own TV, the evening news
with its hooded figures of the Ku Klux Klan
seemed like another movie – *King Solomon's Mines*,
the serial of Atlantis in the sea.
By then I was thirteen,
and no longer went to movies to see movies.
The downstairs forged its attentions forward,
toward the lit horizon, but leaning a little
to one side or the other, arranging the pairs
that would own the county, stores and farms,
        everything
but easy passage out of there –
and through my wing-tipped glasses the balcony

took on a sullen glamor whenever the film
sputtered on the reel, when the music died
and the lights came on, I swiveled my face
up to where they whooped and swore,
to the smoky blue haze and that tribe
of black and brown, licorice, coffee,
taffy, red oak, sweet tea –

wanting to look, not knowing how to see,
I thought it was a special privilege
to enter the side door, climb the stairs
and scan the even rows below – trained bears
in a pit, herded by the stringent rule,
while they were free, lounging above us,
their laughter pelting down on us like trash.

FEATURE
PRESENTATIONS

MEANWHILE

Meanwhile miscegenation laws in 30 states mostly
anti-Negro-and-white plus bills proposed and defeated
but also Chinese-Japanese-Mongolian-Indian-
Hindu-and/or-Filipino(*Malay*)-and-white

> In 1915 *The Birth of a Nation* was shown
> in the White House to Woodrow Wilson
> who may or may not as reported have said *all*

> *so terribly true* but who in 1913 had re-
> segregated federal agencies offices facilities
> dismissed Black workers or put them behind screens

Meanwhile hundreds of thousands
of Blacks arrested on the way to *stop*
for nothing more than on the way

fined what could not pay made
to sign or mark to sign away
back to railroad field mine

chained locked enslaved
again signed away by white
paper white X on black

In 1915 *The Birth of a Nation* – seen by thousands, banned
in some cities, followed by protests, riots in others –
broke all box-office records for decades to come

In 1915 *The Birth of a Nation*
led to the rebirth of the Ku Klux Klan

Meanwhile segregation laws for train cars   streetcars
trashcans   schools   libraries   bathrooms
poolrooms   books
hearses   graveyards   prisons   circus tickets
telephone booths

In 1915, 56 African Americans were lynched,
including William Stanley, who after being
castrated was burned alive over a two-

hour period during which he was lowered
into raised out of lowered into etc. a fire, after

which photographs of the event appeared
on postcards, one with the message:
This is the barbecue we had last night

AN UNMARRIED WOMAN

When I first saw it, I was a high school junior.
  Clayburgh was scandalous
dancing ballet in her tee shirt and panties, showing
  her teenage daughter
a wet spot on the bed after she'd made love to her
  husband, the girl's father,

I was fascinated by her lip gloss and feathered hair.
I had a Fair Isle sweater just like hers and wanted the
  crazy cape
in which she wraps her new lover on a cobblestone
  street in New York.

I didn't understand then, of course, that I would
  someday be divorced
after sixteen years of marriage, just like her character,
  throwing up
on a sidewalk just like she did, jittery in a therapist's
  office,

having an awful blind date, eating dim sum with a
  stranger
who would try to kiss her in a cab. Instead of
  pirouetting
to *Swan Lake*, I jumped around the apartment, singing

43

along with Beyoncé and Pink. Back then, in 1978, I
    didn't quite get
the point. I just liked Jill's outfits – the skirt and tank
    in the final scene
that reminds me now of Sarah Jessica Parker's
    ensemble in the opening credits

of *Sex and the City*. When her artist-lover gives Jill a
    giant painting
as he heads off to Vermont for the summer, and she
    carries it through Soho,
fumbling and twisting in the wind, you can't help but
    root for Jill,

just as I am rooting for myself, watching this movie
    again on DVD
thirty years later, part of my postdivorce Netflix
    recovery.
Jill, today, is in the obituaries. Breast cancer, chronic
    lymphocytic leukemia –

how can that be? She looks so young and fresh as she
    ice-skates
with her pals, runs along the East River where her
    husband steps in dog shit
and blames her. When I first saw *An Unmarried*
    Woman, I went with my friend

and, if I remember correctly, we were freaked out by
     the sex scenes
and barely acknowledged Jill's bland teenage daughter
who would have been about our age. Afterward, at
     Friendly's, we talked

about the pickled herring arc. Jill's lover tells the story
about how his mother threw a jar toward his father's
     head
and how, as he watched the fish smash against the
     wall, he decided

to become an abstract painter. Toward the end of the
     movie,
the lover himself lobs a jar at Jill when she doesn't do
     what he wants.
My friend told me her mother hurled a bottle of
     applesauce at her father

and when she missed, the stuff ruined the wallpaper.
That was just marriage, we guessed, sipping our
     frappes.
We put our hands over our hearts and pledged we'd
     never wed

even as the cute boys came in, crowding into a booth
across from us. We blushed and giggled despite
   ourselves.
Adults, we agreed, were crazy – we wanted no part of
   their messes.

THE BRIDE GOES WILD

You Can't Run Away from It and You Can't Take It
With You, Man of a Thousand Faces: The Children
Upstairs, Brats; All These Women Up in Arms –
Misunderstood Husband Hunters. It Started in
    Paradise –
The Best of Everything: Ten Nights in a Bar Room,
    Men
Without Names, The Exquisite Sinner High and
    Dizzy –
Long Legs, Dimples, The Velvet Touch. Foolin'
    Around,
Just This Once, She Had to Say Yes. A Night to
    Remember.
Don't Tell. I Confess – I'm No Angel, I Am the Law!
The Fiend Who Walked West, Breathless, Accused
My Foolish Heart. The Pleasure of His Company
Changes White Heat to a Cold Wind in August.
But One Night in the Tropics, I Saw What You Did.
Ready, Willing and Able, Naughty but Nice, She Wore
a Yellow Ribbon. Miles from Home, Living It Up,
She Couldn't Say No – My Sister Eileen – Too Young
    to Kiss,
Each Pearl a Tear. The Awful Truth: Ladies Love
    Brutes.
The Good News: The Devil Is a Sissy. So Tickle Me,

Doctor X, Truly Madly Deeply. Keep Laughing. You
    Gotta
Stay Happy. Naked, the Invisible Woman Cries and
    Whispers
Nothing but the Truth, Too Scared to Scream.

THE BLUE ANGEL

Marlene Dietrich is singing a lament
for mechanical love.
She leans against a mortarboard tree
on a plateau by the seashore.

She's a life-sized toy,
the doll of eternity;
her hair is shaped like an abstract hat
made out of white steel.

Her face is powdered, whitewashed and
immobile like a robot.
Jutting out of her temple, by an eye,
is a little white key.

She gazes through dull blue pupils
set in the whites of her eyes.
She closes them, and the key
turns by itself.

She opens her eyes, and they're blank
like a statue's in a museum.
Her machine begins to move, the key turns
again, her eyes change, she sings

– you'd think I would have thought a plan
to end the inner grind,
but not till I have found a man
to occupy my mind.

ROPE

Cut a Throat Week? Strangulation Day?
He isn't joking, but don't believe a word.
The master of misdirection, of slaughtered stars
and undercover blondes, has tricked us again:
he's made us think this film's about a murder.

Look closer. It's 1948,
and two young men in tasteful suits, who share
this vast, immaculate apartment, men
who bicker like old marrieds, are having a party.
Inside the chest, the body of their friend,
the party guest who isn't really missing.
Oh yes, there's been a murder –

                                              but what's inside
the chest is simpler, more damning: a secret.
They've shut their secret in a chest, but failed
to lock it. They've covered it with damask, lit
candles on it, served the dinner from it.
All the party guests are tainted with it.

And when their mentor reaches for the hasp,
they don't make a move to stop him. They wait,
almost eager, flushed and out of breath,
as he opens the lid, exposes the thing
that they so feared, so longed for him to see.

JULIANA GRAY (1972–)   51

ART MOVIES: *THE AGONY AND THE ECSTASY*

I learned a lot from this one, too. You have
to wreck, completely, your first fresco. Next,
you head up to the mountain top and see
the Sistine Chapel ceiling in the clouds,
and then – you're on your back in agony.
The ecstasy is when the Pope goes back
to bed. "When will you finish it?" He asks
a million times, "When will you finish it?"

Charlton, way up there on the scaffolding,
painting with chocolate pudding, so that when
it falls into his mouth it's pleasurable.
You're fine with this, except you don't like Charlton.
A charioteer, okay, a genius, no.
Who do you want, you snob, Peter O'Toole?

Ben Hur was good, maybe a little long.
Do you know that the author of *Ben Hur*,
Lew Wallace, was a Union general
and later governor of New Mexico?

The thing is, no one lived there then – nobody.
He was the governor of maybe twelve
Or thirteen guys – the governor of nothing!

When will I finish it, your Holiness?

I'm thinking I could make a little skylight
by banging my head against the ceiling, hard.

IMITATION OF LIFE

So what if I've seen it
a half-dozen times,
when that movie crops up
in mid-afternoon or the middle

of the night, I'm drawn to the tv
as if I have nothing better to do,
as if my life depends on seeing
two daughters betray their mothers,

then live to regret it.
And I'm not talking about
the refined black and white original
with Claudette Colbert and Louise Beavers,

the version where the daughter
who looks white but is black
is actually played by an actress
who looked white but was black.

Her name? Fredi Washington,
and she was lovely enough
to be a star, but Hollywood
had no clue what to do with

a black actress whose light skin
would make her look silly
in a maid's uniform. No, the version
that hooks me every time

is the gaudy Technicolor remake,
a film stopped in its tracks
whenever Madam Lana Turner
appears on screen, her blond coiffure

fancy whether her character's rich
or poor, hourglass figure emphasized
even when she's supposed to be
a dowdy widow with no funds,

a stage actress wannabe.
In this version, like the first,
a black woman and a white woman
move in together to raise

their daughters, fend off poverty.
But all Lana cares about
is becoming a star, so her black friend
really raises both girls –

who grow up to be Sandra Dee
and an actress who looks like Natalie Wood,
but isn't, a white woman playing
at being a black girl

who looks white. It's she
who truly fascinates – her
performance pouty, impetuous,
not merely tragic like Fredi Washington's,

but so blatant you forget Lana's
in the movie, so histrionic
I laugh out loud whenever this
Natalie Wood look-alike screams

she wants to be *white, white, white*
because that's exactly what she is!
I can't resist the scene where she's
run away from home, joined

a chorus line, finally able to pass as white,
dancing at a seedy club for dollars a week.
So thrilled is she not to be called
Sarah Jane – a colored girl's name if ever

there was one – that she rejects her mother,
her long-suffering, dark-skinned mother,
lets her fellow chorus girls think
she was raised by a mammy, a Negro cook.

I can't help roaring with abrupt laughter
at the end when the Natalie Wood look-alike
returns, stumbling back home, knowing somehow
her mother was dead, stung by her daughter's

spite. The funeral's fantastic, attended
by every black Central Casting could find,
complete with gospel solo by Mahalia Jackson
herself. When Sarah Jane comes running in

to sprawl across her poor dead mother's
casket, clawing at the coffin lid, crying
copious tears, sputtering that she really
did love her mother, I'm nearly convulsed

by these hilarious Hollywood ironies,
such delicious contradictions. I'm always
left wondering whose life this movie
is an imitation of, whose version

of black and white, mother and daughter.
Certainly not mine or yours, not anyone's
with sense enough to know tearjerker
movies are like cotton candy –

something that looks like
nourishment but isn't,
concoctions too cloying
to ever be good for you.

AUBADE

At eight a.m. what could be better
than Bette Davis starring in "The Letter,"

with Herbert Marshall and his ever-puckered lips
as her loyal husband, Mr. Pussy-Whipped.

Here's the story in a nutshell: it's
Malaya, it's hot, Bette Davis has this itch

only sexy Geoff can scratch. But he marries
"that native woman!" What a catastrophe

for Bette, so she shoots him a few times
and when the cops come she offers gin & lime

and says Geoff tried to force himself on her.
What else could she do? Her honor

was at stake. Of course. The trial should be a breeze.
Until an unctuous clerk and part-time leech

produces her incriminating letter
proving Geoff was not a drunken lecher.

Money changes hands, Bette is acquitted.
Then Herbert Marshall learns his wife's a bitch.

He cries like the douche bag he is and forgives
Bette who's fed up and ready for the shiv.

Gladly she steps into the moon-shady
garden where she's stabbed by the Dragon Lady.

The credits roll. The End. I stand and stretch.
Outside, the day is black-and-white, a sketch

of the afternoon to come. There are bills
to pay, errands that have to be run (pills

from Rite-Aid, shirts from Clean & Brite
and someone in a truck to fix my satellite).

There must be twenty things I need to get done,
but look what's on next! It's "Mr. Skeffington."

CASABLANCA

As years unwind now reels unwind.
Gray springs out of the hair,
cheeks refill, and eyelids lighten.
Bogie, beautifully indifferent,
seduces a cigarette and womankind.

Ingrid, in perilous rain
intensified by angle shots,
is Juno, fair and fair.
Where France falls and gates clang shut
she faithfully misses the final train.

Now Vichy is dead, and Peter Lorre
less cowardly, and Greenstreet
has gone with the parrot,
and I knew a boy with sandy hair
could do the dialogue all blurry;

cigarette dangling, cheeks sucked hollow,
hands in his jacket pockets,
could do the dialogue
for drinks at any party;
went down with his destroyer, swallowed

in the other half of that real war.
The tough guy, lately dead
of cancer, holds the girl and then they kiss
for the last time, and time goes west
and we come back to where we really are.

VARIATION ON A THEME
BY RIDLEY SCOTT

In *Blade Runner* smoke seems to hover
everywhere, & despite the aura of lit up billboards
& brilliant windows, night might as well be perpetual

like the rain. Sure, it's supposed to be L.A.;
it's supposed to be 2019, too,
but it may well have been the Village, 1985,
the year they showed that film every Friday at
        midnight,

the year I exited the Waverly Cinema onto Sixth Ave
& into downpour. No thunder.
The girl who was supposed to join me, the one

whom I'd imagined for weeks, imagined kissing . . .
the one whose name I no longer remember,
never showed, though there was a phone message
        waiting
at home. No matter

how young I was
I knew better than to think the showers might cleanse
    that hurt,
the way Detective Deckard walked
those fictional streets as if stalked by his own horror.

How much protection can a trench coat afford?

In the movie the replicants are all trying
to live longer – in other words they're just like us –
& it's Roy, designed to kill,
who, before he dies – Is it of natural causes? –
tells us that what he's seen will be gone with him.

This is why we write it all down
& why old photos stand flat & mute on Deckard's
    piano
& why Rachel, a replicant herself, is so confused.
She, also, has photos, has stories she can no longer
    believe:

The girl she thought she was
was someone else. So I think of all the little lies
I've tried to live
because in the end memory is just steam wafting

on a rainy night, the white billows visible
in the flow of a hundred windows in bloom. In the
        movie
& in that city some were trying
to remember & others longing to forget

& there was enough blame to assign to anyone who
        wanted.
I could say something overly romantic & sentimental

right now, suggest I walked toward dawn
because I was 17 & thought every slight was dramatic.
Or I could claim my best Casanova,
say I met another woman – Beth – & she took me
        home
& modesty prevents me from saying more.

Which would you believe when it comes down to faith
in the end, comes down to what's beyond the camera's
        frame?

GERRY LAFEMINA (1968–)   65

SOLILOQUY WITH HONEY: TIME TO DIE

A box arrived today filled with honeys and a DVD,
Blade Runner, a beautiful violent movie.   In the letter,
my friend chides me for looking away from violence.
He's right, but I wonder whether turning away
is an act of resistance rather than cowardice, but
        because
I've cared for two people through death, watching
as one's jaw slid down out of its hinge sideways
like a cartoon corpse, does not mean I know anything.
Blade Runner enacts the question of what it means
to be fully human. Replicant Roy Batty, embedded
with memories, gives a monologue, which has entered
the popular lexicon: *I've seen C-beams glitter,* he said,
and, *I've seen things you people wouldn't believe.*
Intelligent, handsome, struggling with emerging
        emotion,
he is real, yet temporary, despised, though the
        protagonist
comes to understand Roy is just like us in the end.
I wonder if honeys are like memory – *all these moments –*
                distilled
from the places they came from. There are five in all
from different countries – including one from
        Morocco
which I open first, dipping a pinky and tipping it

to my daughter's mouth. *It tastes full of light crystals*,
she exclaims, and I realize I am growing hungry
for what seems to be essentialized only through
        residues
of bodies that have lived and died,
leaving something
of themselves behind
off which I must learn to feed.

ENTER THE DRAGON
Los Angeles, CA, 1976

For me, the movie starts with a black man
Leaping into an orbit of badges, tiny moons

Catching the sheen of his perfect black afro.
Arc kicks, karate chops, and thirty cops

On their backs. It starts with the swagger,
The cool lean into the leather front seat

Of the black and white he takes off in.
Deep hallelujahs of moviegoers drown

Out the *wah wah* guitar. Salt & butter
High-fives, *Right on, brother!* and Daddy

Glowing so bright he can light the screen
All by himself. This is how it goes down.

Friday night and my father drives us
Home from the late show, two heroes

Cadillacking across King Boulevard.
In the car's dark cab, we jab and clutch,

Jim Kelly and Bruce Lee with popcorn
Breath, and almost miss the lights flashing

In the cracked side mirror. I know what's
Under the seat, but when the uniforms

Approach from the rear quarter panel,
When the fat one leans so far into my father's

Window I can smell his long day's work,
When my father – this John Henry of a man –

Hides his hammer, doesn't buck, tucks away
His baritone, license and registration shaking as if

Showing a bathroom pass to a grade school
Principal, I learn the difference between cinema

And city, between the moviehouse cheers
Of old men and the silence that gets us home.

JOHN MURILLO (1971–)   69

SHANE

There was no moon & the horizon a fire breaking
over the black earth & the man on horseback floated
into the red plum of the sky & did not hear the boy
screaming his name & then there was only the earth
& the sky like a clay sea & the boy who believed
it was his imperfection the man was leaving.

My father always slept in movies & we walked home
under the trees & stars without talking & there is
an understanding between fathers & sons & death is
not something a boy can understand & my father was
    dying
out of his body as I was growing into mine &
    there was
only the black earth & pale summer sky & the horizon
like a fire breaking on our heads.

THE JAMES BOND MOVIE

The popcorn is greasy, and I forgot to bring a
    Kleenex.
A pill that's a bomb inside the stomach of a man inside

The Embassy blows up. Eructations of flame,
    luxurious
cauliflowers giganticize into motion. The entire 29-ft

screen is orange, is crackling flesh and brick bursting,
blackening, smithereened. I unwrap a Dentyne and,
    while

jouncing my teeth in rubber tongue-smarting
    clove, try
with the 2-inch-wide paper to blot butter off my
    fingers.

A bubble-bath, room-sized, in which 14 girls,
    delectable
and sexless, twist-topped Creamy Freezes (their
    blonde,

red, brown, pinkish, lavender or silver wiglets all
screwed that high, and varnished), scrub-tickle a lone

male, whose chest has just the right amount and
    distribu-
tion of curly hair. He's nervously pretending to defend

his modesty. His crotch, below the waterline, is also
below the frame – but unsubmerged all 28 slick foamy
    boobs.

Their makeup fails to let the girls look naked.
    Caterpil-
lar lashes, black and thick, lush lips glossed pink like

the gum I pop and chew, contact lenses on the eyes
    that are
mostly blue, they're nose-perfect replicas of each
    other.

I've got most of the grease off and onto this little
    square
of paper. I'm folding it now, making creases with my
    nails.

TAKE TWO: *BONNIE & CLYDE* /
DASHBOARD SCENE

passenger seat   arrows   boots on the dashboard
cowboy toes and frayed heels   but women's boots
leather-laced   and it's a truck   on the left

steering wheel on the left too   long mid-western
road forks ahead   [pan]   circles   maybe a gyre
a dark steel quonset hut   black-and-white magpies

she rides shotgun   feet on the dashboard
asks   *did my mother do this at my age   did yours*
arrows are invisible   yet there   they prick her flesh

radio gone   truck speeds by   if she is smoking
we can't see or smell it   but we know   in her lap
[dolly shot]   she cradles the guns

          what is down the dotted line of the road
is this Bonnie   is that Clyde driving the wrong
side   yes   [master shot]   they don't know   now

even closer   magpies   they croon
how someone *lies over the ocean*   croon 'til they see
a road block ahead   *stop*   she cries   *stop now*

SUSAN TERRIS (1937–)   73

THE PRISONER OF ZENDA

At the end a
The Prisoner of Zenda,
The King being out of danger,
Stewart Granger
(As Rudolf Rassendyll)
Must swallow a bitter pill
By renouncing his co-star,
Deborah Kerr.

It would be poor behavia
In him and in Princess Flavia
Were they to put their own
Concerns before those of the Throne.
Deborah Kerr must wed
The King instead.

Rassendyll turns to go.
Must it be so?
Why can't they have their cake
And eat it, for heaven's sake?
Please let them have it both ways,
The audience prays.
And yet it is hard to quarrel
With a plot so moral.

One redeeming factor,
However, is that the actor
Who plays the once-dissolute King
(Who has learned through suffering
Not to drink or be mean
To his future Queen),
Far from being a stranger,
Is *also* Stewart Granger.

MORE STARS THAN
IN HEAVEN

POEM ENDING WITH A SENTENCE BY HEATH LEDGER

Each grinding flattened American vowel smashed to
centerlessness, his glee that whatever long ago mutilated his

mouth, he has mastered to mutilate

you: the Joker's voice, so unlike
the bruised, withheld, wounded voice of Ennis Del Mar.

Once I have the voice

that's
the line

and at

the end
of the line

is a hook

and attached
to that

is the soul.

FOR INGRID BERGMAN

I first loved you in '58
in the back of the auditorium –
while the other students fidgeted
or whispered in the dark, I was rapt,
yours from the opening frame.

It didn't matter that you were a nun,
and that Bing, as the new pastor,
was the one you loved – you held love in
and at the end left, tubercular
and undeclared, but rarefied
by that burning, a glow of a kind
that seemed to say love would be
like this, an impossible giving
beyond our arms' poor reach . . .
And though the film shone dully
as all those lives of saints,
though the reels, as usual,
swelled and skipped,
your scenes had a luster,
a finish on the light,
and from that time on
light has always owed much
to your beatific gaze,
the half turn and long look beyond . . .

Next, St. Michael spoke to you
in the winds over Orléans,
in the bright spikes of clouds –
I saw your flower-perfect mouth
respond, as if to sun, above the smoke
of your sack robe and cropped hair,
above your flame-white skin,
the fires that could not finally
take your heart . . .

        And this September,
with its weak sun white through the grey,
takes me back to those years where
I was groomed religiously for loss
and a lovely countenance . . . or where
Bogart walked away empty into the fog,
that light and hopelessness in your eyes.
I understood when Gary Cooper died
in that Spanish pass so you might go on –
always, something more exacting than love,
always, someone was losing you . . .

And so today
with rain in the afternoon,
life again in black and white,

I recall my first memory of you
and how more purely than anything
I've ever seen, your face said *love*,
still says it now, far across the dark
and diminished vision of our years . . .

FATTY ARBUCKLE

*Roscoe "Fatty" Arbuckle's career came to an abrupt end
in 1921 after he was charged with manslaughter in the
death of Virginia Rappe, a young starlet who was along
for a Labor Day orgy he hosted in San Francisco.*
                                            – The Movie Book

The City Council of Minneapolis,
because of his crime of passion,
voted to ban him from their theaters.
When Paramount refused to release
his last picture in 1921, *that* America
received the news with great
indifference.

*The alley is still there
down which a portly, disheveled
figure fled in the early hours.*
The bedclothes had been dragged
from the two mattresses
and set afire at the head
of the stairs.

Fatty got his start at the age
of eight, appearing nightly
in black face with a stock

company in Kansas City.
At the end, forty-six, amid
rumors of more showgirls,
he died in his sleep.

People adored him
for *The Gangsters*, *Ben's Kid*,
and *Gasoline Gus.* One
of his ex-wives said he was always
an embarrassment: just an obese
uncle, beloved of millions,
a buffoon to those who knew him.

For a time he took the name
Will B. Good and became a director
in New York. That he was acquitted
after the third trial did
not matter.

Witnesses claimed Arbuckle came
out of the room – these depositions
of sexual conquest and its attendant
failure! – dressed in pajamas
and wearing Miss Rappe's Panama
hat cocked on the side of his head.
On his face, that fatuous grin.

JANET LEIGH IS AFRAID OF JAZZ
For Eddie Muller

The voices that swim through the music
offering something forbidden, close-up,
the dark arms of the horn player, his skin
fitting him sleek as a shark suit, clasping
the sax lifting it as sound descends
in long sizzling lines like wires arcing out,
empty eye sliding up and back
to the halo of the spot, motes drifting.
It makes her want to run. Like it could tear her
apart, a man at each limb lifting her
off the bed at the Otay Mesa motel,
all of them dressed in black and the music
never letting up its dazzling spun-out
phrases. If she could run, she would, under
the shadowy arcade as the camera pans wide
but she's hobbled by her tight skirt,
the staccato of high heels tapping
a rhythm on the uneven street,
her breasts heaving under cashmere,
dogcollar of pearls around her perfect
neck while the sea crashes in the near
distance. We know she's doomed by music,
cloudburst of percussion on the windshield
then silence, the camera wheels around

and Bates Motel appears, lit up on the sign.
It's the way every aperture turns
into another eye and the shower
won't stop running until long after
she's died. We know she's doomed, chords
shifting darkly, but she persists,
carrying on with her share of sorrow,
changing into black lingerie and
skipping town if she has to, ending
finally there, wherever the
heart of trouble happens to be.

DEAR JOHN WAYNE

August and the drive-in picture is packed.
We lounge on the hood of the Pontiac
surrounded by the slow-burning spirals they sell
at the window, to vanquish the hordes of mosquitoes.
Nothing works. They break through the smoke screen
     for blood.

Always the lookout spots the Indians first,
spread north to south, barring progress.
The Sioux or some other Plains bunch
in spectacular columns, ICBM missiles,
feathers bristling in the meaningful sunset.

The drum breaks. There will be no parlance.
Only the arrows whining, a death-cloud of nerves
swarming down on the settlers
who die beautifully, tumbling like dust weeds
into the history that brought us all here
together: this wide screen beneath the sign of the bear.

The sky fills, acres of blue squint and eye
that the crowd cheers. His face moves over us,
a thick cloud of vengeance, pitted
like the land that was once flesh. Each rut,

each scar makes a promise: *It is*
not over, this fight, not as long as you resist.

Everything we see belongs to us.

A few laughing Indians fall over the hood
slipping in the hot spilled butter.
The eye sees a lot, John, but the heart is so blind.
Death makes us owners of nothing.
He smiles, a horizon of teeth
the credits reel over, and then the white fields

again blowing in the true-to-life dark.
The dark films over everything.
We get into the car
scratching our mosquito bites, speechless and small
as people are when the movie is done.
We are back in our skins.

How can we help but keep hearing his voice,
the flip side of the sound track, still playing:
Come on, boys, we got them
where we want them, drunk, running.
They'll give us what we want, what we need.
Even his disease was the idea of taking everything.
Those cells, burning, doubling, splitting out of their
     skins.

CELEBRITY STALKING

The celebrities are at it again. They keep
stalking me for poetry. Just the other day
George Clooney tried to deliver a pizza
so I could sign his broadside, Meryl Streep
crouched in my back yard with a first edition
in hand, Julia Roberts broke into my bathroom
to ask about pentameter, and Charlie Sheen left
twenty-six voicemails asking for *sexstinas*
written in the colloquial language of porn,
but these movie stars think they know the real me
behind the poetry because they read tabloids
in line at the super market that detail
the lurid private lives of poets who take lovers,
get caught without make-up, carry small dogs,
enjoy gay trysts, drink absinthe, and own
many-chambered homes with deep-pile
cream carpets, secret rooms, and libraries
the size of Luxembourg. They couldn't know
that I'm allergic to even numbers and no longer
fluent in filthy words. I'm feeling inflamed
on this spring nocturnal in the City of Angels,
a hundred-watt moon on the rise and songbirds
playing their music well past prime time
like neighbors with no children. No moment,
no poet ever safe from the paparazzi,

so we duck into seedy bars while tourists
mug with our tread-upon stars inlaid
along Hollywood Boulevard.

HUD

If a starched white shirt clings to his broad wet chest
and deer and antelope play,
it must be Texas.
Dust, highways and diners serving
very bad coffee.

Look at those teasing eyes.
Smell the smoke's slow curl
into bright sun,
Can this tale be told today?

Where else can a man be a jerk
and still make a woman's heart ache?

We want more.
More of his cool, patrician inspection
of the very core of our lusting selves.

Oh for a day to be Patricia Neal
warming up her whiskey voice
just so she can tell Paul Newman
where to go and how fast to get there.

Just watch the sun fall behind the horizon
casting out the will of God and urging the rise

of demons: drugs, dollars,
the fleeting power of men in uniform
come to kick ass,
and drag the beautiful, the mild, the musical
across piney wood floors
of tract houses and suburban drawl.

The South on the verge of existentialism.
With evil enough to require regret and redemption.
God in a thousand carry-ons
in film reels to come.

For now the jerk stands bare chested
literate, tasty.

TO HARPO MARX

O Harpo! When did you seem like an angel
   the last time?
   and played the gray harp of gold?

When did you steal the silverware
   and bug-spray the guests?

When did your brother find rain
   in your sunny courtyard?

When did you chase your last blonde
   across the Millionairesses' lawn
   with a bait hook on a line
   protruding from your bicycle?

Or when last you powderpuffed
   your white flour face
   with fishbarrel cover?

Harpo! Who was that Lion
   I saw you with?

How did you treat the midget
   and Konk the giant?

Harpo, in your recent nightclub appearance
   in New Orleans were you old?
   Were you still chiding with your horn
   in the cane at your golden belt?

Did you still emerge from your pockets
   another Harpo, or screw on
   new wrists?

Was your vow of silence an Indian Harp?

JULY 13 [from *The Daily Mirror*]

I'm going to miss you, Robert Mitchum,
as I make my rounds in lower Manhattan
checking the progress of Joe DiMaggio's
56-game hitting streak the way you did
in *Farewell, My Lovely*. Next to Bogart
you were the best Philip Marlowe. Smart,
too. Getting arrested for marijuana use the
year I was born was a shrewd career move.
Sleepless by instinct, you looked like
a car mechanic and were a fighter whose best
moment came when he got off the canvas
and took another punch. You lost every fight
with the woman in the houseboat who sang
"There's a fire down below in my heart."
She came out of the past and now at last
you've joined her in some South American
beach where escaped convicts dream
of going, and I'm walking on Sixth Avenue
with your groggy voice in my mind
daring the world to surprise you.

DAVID LEHMAN (1948–)   95

THE FAKE TEARS OF SHIRLEY TEMPLE

How many sets of her parents are dead. How
many times over is she an orphan. A plane,
a crosswalk, a Boer war. A childbirth, of course,
her childbirth. When she, Shirley Temple, came
out of her mother, plump even at her corners
like a bag of goldfish, and one pinhole just one
pinhole necessary. Shirley Temple, cry for us,
and Shirley Temple cried. The first word of no
baby is "Hello," how strange. The baby believes,
"I was here before you, learning to wave just
    like the Atlantic." Alone in the world
just like the Atlantic, and left on a doorstep
just like the Atlantic, wrapped in the grayest,
roughest blanket. Shirley Temple gurgled
and her first words were, "Your father is lost
at sea." "Your mother was thrown by a foam-
colored horse." "Your father's round face is
a round set of ripples." "Every gull has a chunk
    of your mom in its beak."
Shirley Temple what makes you cry. What do
you think of to make you cry. Mommies stand
in a circle and whisper to her. "Shirley Temple
there will be war. Shirley Temple you'll get no
lunch." Dry, and dry, and a perfect desert. Then:
    "Shirley Temple your goldfish are dead,

they are swimming toward the ocean even now,"
    and her tears they fall in black
and white, and her tears they star in the movie.
She cries so wet her hair uncurls, and then the rag
is in the ringlet and the curl is in the wave, she thinks
of dimples tearing out of her cheeks and just running,
out of cheeks knees and elbows and running hard
back to the little creamy waves where they belong,
and the ocean. Her first
    glimpse of the ocean was a fake tear for dad.
A completely filled eye for her unseen dead father,
who when he isn't dead he is gone across the water.

HARPO MARX

Harpo Marx, your hands white-feathered the harp –
the only words you ever spoke were sound.
The movie's not always the sick man of the arts,
yours touched the stars; Harpo, your motion picture
is still life unchanging, not nature dead.
You dumbly memorized an unwritten script ...
I saw you first two years before you died,
a black-and-white fall, near Fifth in Central Park:
old blond hair too blonder, old eyes too young.
Movie trucks and five police trucks wheel to wheel
like covered wagons. The crowd as much or little.
I wish I had knelt ... I age to your wincing smile,
like Dante's movie, the great glistening wheel of life –
the genius *happy* ... a generic actor.

THE DEATH OF MARILYN MONROE

The ambulance men touched her cold
body, lifted it, heavy as iron,
onto the stretcher, tried to close
the mouth, closed the eyes, tied the
arms to the side, moved a caught
strand of hair, as if it mattered,
saw the shape of her breasts, flattened by
gravity, under the sheet,
carried her, as if it were she,
down the steps.

These men were never the same. They went out
afterwards, as they always did,
for a drink or two, but they could not meet
each other's eyes.

                        Their lives took
a turn – one had nightmares, strange
pains, impotence, depression. One did not
like his work, his wife looked
different, his kids. Even death
seemed different to him – a place where she
would be waiting,

and one found himself standing at night
in the doorway to a room of sleep, listening to a
woman breathing, just an ordinary
woman
breathing.

100 SHARON OLDS (1942–)

YOU, JOHN WAYNE

Sonofagun! In whose wake is silence!

O leathery centaur! You flash over the purple
   horizon on a sun-bronco with a thundering
   rib-cage, snorting fire, spurred by the
   fastest gun west of the Pecos.

All us American kids
who love Death
love you, John Wayne,
because You Made Good
and, unlike niggers and jews,
You Have Guts!
Your blazing guns still the bad man's lusty
   aliveness. Look how quietly he sprawls on
   the blood-stained ground! O kill him again!
Shoot the nesters, greasers, horse-thieves and
   cattle rustlers. The crows peck their eyeballs
   in the scrub and the sage brush.

All the others may cop out
but you, John Wayne, will go on shooting,
smiling, cool,
without unseemly passion.

Shoot the blonde, true blue as the yellow rose
    of Texas, whom you won in a poker game in a
    Dodge City saloon.
Shoot her father the ranch-owner.
Shoot the sheriff.
Shoot the posse.
Shoot the birds out of the sky.
Shoot the mountain cats in their dark hollows.

Sonofagun! gatherer of darkness and silence.
Rider into the bloody sunset.
Emptiness like a wind rushes in behind you.

102 WILLIAM PILLIN (1910–85)

AN APOLOGY FOR TRASHING
MAGAZINES IN WHICH YOU APPEAR

I was out of line, Brad Pitt.
You're no Eliot Spitzer.
I'm no preacher. This apology no bully pulpit
where I sermonize our epitasis –
Woody Allen tragicomedy in which I play
    "Serendipity,"
and am blinded by you, a star, Jupiter

(third brightest in the night, spitting
image of the sky god). *Patience* might be for pipits
and "forever" a spit
of land neighboring Atlantis, but I'll wait my turn.
    Pity
your first marriage ended. I didn't mind her as much
    as that Jolie-Pitt
situation, complete with pitter-

patter of 12 *Benetton*-inspired feet. But, I'm not bitter.
    My pit
bull bears your name, and I call my man – with whom
    I'm going to Pittsburgh
for a wedding – out his name. Into yours: Brad Pitt.
Daydreams of you and me rivaled only by Brandon
    and me on *Peach Pit*

counters, from the original *90210*. Even so, I'd wish he
    were you. Adonis epitome.
Abandon Hollywood for Bed-Stuy, skip down spit-

paved sidewalks to my brownstone. My poetry
    pittance,
your movie money ... I suspect we'd do fine with our
    combined capital.
We'd be the mixed-race Pitts
on Tompkins Park. I'd be hospitable,
hosting meet and greets so as not to appear uppity.
Casually introducing you, I'd say, "Oh, this is Brad.
    This is just Brad Pitt."

You'd find macabre humor in my obsession with
    Poe's *Pit*
and the Pendulum and the palpitating
Tell-Tale Heart. The heart is an odd organ, a maudlin
    muscle, a cesspit
of undeserved affection. I admit I've had trouble
    pitting
good sense against non, but who hasn't? (Did you
    know the per capita
divorce rate is 50%? Pitiful.)

Like with Juliette and Jennifer, I pray Angelina was
    a pit
stop on your way to Brooklyn. When I first saw you,
    Brad Pitt,
I was 15 and became so ill I was rushed to the
    hospital.
My hands, feet and armpits
began to sweat as if I were riding horseback up a hill
    toward a love who made the pit
of my stomach ache; literally, *Legends of the Fall* was
    my pitfall.

Brad Pitt, I imagine a much older you – spitfire
and only slightly decrepit – staring my epitaph
down as if your gaze were the capital and my
    headstone a ghetto to be pitied.

THE GARBOS AND DIETRICHS

Moving like a dream through Ibiza
through midnight cities of the world
buying dreams of men/and their hearts
to hang at dressing tables, how many ornaments
to wear for dinner, or selfish supper parties –

this sin does not show by candlelight, their children
do not hear that cry in the night, odd pregnancies
abortions are not counted, smashed faces
wrenched hearts left behind at harborside
when their ships pull out.

I speak of suicides, men dropped at tide.
I speak of sleeping pills that still our aching mind.
I speak of lovers they murdered because they are so
        kind.
Anything to stay beautiful and remain blind
to those men they turn into swine.

B MOVIES &
BIT PLAYERS

TO LON CHANEY IN *THE UNKNOWN*

The circus knows that animals are not infants,
but laws.

Lon, armless knife thrower, your Spanish hat
judges the hard silence.

Your natural arms not gone, but bound.
When Nanon, the inchoate
Joan Crawford, said that she felt imperially safe
in your non-arms, your fanaticism
believed, bribed a surgeon, returned you

in triumph to horror, her: subsumed
in the Strong Man's vast,
hairy appendages. Your brain a storm
of hoops, condemned tents,
hushed deaths of the quadripedal. Dear

Lon,
Nanon did not love you for your missing
arms, your arms loved you missing.

The Unknown needs no arms. Only the blade
inside the blade, the sternness.

MOVIE EXTRAS

They are always falling into crevasses,
Misstepping into wobbles of quicksand
Or marching as foot soldiers over the world's
Edge to prove some tyrannical point.

Even with animals they are unlucky,
Snake-bitten, piranha-gnawed, mauled
By abominables, and the commonest dog
Turning on them as on evil.

If disaster follows them like a cloud,
The heavens burst, and they are
Borne away clinging, poor wretches,
To none but each other,

It is always so hero and heroine
Can come stepping blithely
Over mines and springes and rubble,
Stealing our hearts, wearing our faces.

Movie after movie, day after day
They die almost out of earshot,
Just beyond our affections,
Easily, without fanfare.

Who are they, these strange expendables –
Victims of spectacular meteors,
Scorpions, cars recklessly driven, wars –
That the world should love to do them in?

They pass anonymously in the street,
Lean idly in doorways. Before the knife
Plunges, the bullet hits, they say:
Do not pity us, we could be anyone.

SAM

When the Fat Man walks in the door,
Does Sam know this means his buddy
Has just sold his services for a handshake?
Or that he's about to lose the ten percent
Rick gave him for his 'tude and his tunes,

And what's the difference now between
The piano and the man, the music,
And the potted plants? I'd like to think
An artist like Sam, maybe he'd toss
The contents of a shot glass in

The Fat Man's face, though we can
Assume it's a stand in for Rick,
For love, for the ways friendship
And loyalty can bite, a splash of
Acid reserved for kiss-offs.

And then walk, the way he
Cake-walked in 1917 out of Harlem
With the troops and the band
Through France, to Paris,
Who called his blues genius

And doesn't give a shit who he eats
And sleeps with, free enough
To persuade him to skip the trip
Back home, a man like that will always
Pack his pride, and when

The Fat Man says
A deal's a deal, well,
You know how we Negros get
When white folk act like they
Messing with a child

And forget they're dealing
With a man.

THE DEATH OF CARMEN MIRANDA

Dying on television,
on *The Jimmy Durante Show*,
spinning another samba for the tourists,
she staggered beneath the banana headdress
and dropped to one knee.
The audience began to giggle
at the wobbly pyramid of bananas,
but the comedian with the fat nose and the fedora
growled *Stop the music!* and lifted her up.
I cannot find my breath, Carmen said,
fingers fanning across her chest.
The mouth of the camera opened
to chuckle at her accent, but then
widened into an astonished *Oh*.

Later that night, at the mansion,
her maid found Carmen sleeping without breath,
could not unlock the mirror from her fingers.
The hair no one saw on television was unpinned,
grown long beneath the banana headdress,
bleached yellow like the bananas.

CURSE OF THE CAT WOMAN

It sometimes happens
that the woman you meet and fall in love with
is of that strange Transylvanian people
with an affinity for cats.

You take her to a restaurant, say, or a show,
on an ordinary date, being attracted
by the glitter in her slitty eyes and her catlike walk,
and afterwards of course you take her in your arms
and she turns into a black panther
and bites you to death.

Or perhaps you are saved in the nick of time
and she is tormented by the knowledge of her
        tendency:
That she daren't hug a man
unless she wants to risk clawing him up.

This puts you both in a difficult position –
panting lovers who are prevented from touching
not by bars but by circumstance:
You have terrible fights and say cruel things
for having the hots does not give you a sweet temper.

One night you are walking down a dark street
and hear the pad-pad of a panther following you,
but when you turn around there are only shadows,
or perhaps one shadow too many.

You approach, calling, "Who's there?"
and it leaps on you.
Luckily you have brought along your sword
and you stab it to death.

And before your eyes it turns into the woman you
        love,
her breast impaled on your sword,
her mouth dribbling blood saying she loved you
but couldn't help her tendency.

So death released her from the curse at last,
and you knew from the angelic smile on her dead face
that in spite of a life the devil owned,
love had won, and heaven pardoned her.

THE HORROR SHOW

The house possessed, the hero impotent,
the sleuth vanishing half way through the plot,
the demon at it for its own sake, no money
involved, pure hate, I reach for you.
"Honey, it's all loose ends. Let's get out."
"It's not art, I know," you say. The floor blisters
and swallows dog and children. Blood runs
    downstairs.
"Let's go home," I whisper. "This is stupid."
The priest vomits, his cross inverted. "You go,"
you say. "You always want to *talk*. It's not
worth it." Satan with the face of a doberman
rapes a baby as I'm swallowed by my seat.

THREE HORSE OPERAS
for Patti Smith

At the end of Bing Crosby's *Riding High* his horse
Will be buried in the clay of the racetrack where he fell,
As a lesson for all of us. Sad, waggish Bing,
The Mob didn't want Broadway Bill to win, so the jockey
Pulled on the reins until the thoroughbred, straining
Over the finish line first, collapsed, heart attack.

I loved you like a guitar string breaking
Under the conviction of a clumsy hand –
Something like that . . . I suppose I must have
Been thinking of you and your complex and beautiful
        band,
Except the image demands I hold the guitar,
If not you, and the broken string, as

Over and over loudspeakers call riders to the starting
        gate.
The track bartender and a teller, a sharpshooter and
        the chess master
Wrestler, the petty con man and a cop, reprise their
        parts.
The heist gang dons clown masks, and
Sherry will betray George, and Johnny can't love Fay,
And the fortune in the suitcase just blows away.

118 ROBERT POLITO (1951–)

HARRY DEAN STANTON IS DYING

"The sun is dying out." – HDS (from PARTLY
FICTION)

See it in the crow-black eyes, the stubble
And the way his lids sag as he belts out

The next sad song. Jack Nicholson's gone
For good, an empty husk at the bottom

Of the push cart. My daughter Skypes
From the Cancer Ward in a Guatemalan

Children's Hospital, something about a boy
Named Lester who has no parents, no relatives,

Lester in a cancer-riddled body, only a matter
Of time before the next Mexican ranchera comes on.

Lester who misses his roommate who's gone
For specialized treatment in the United States,

Lester of the non-sequiturs: a man walking
Out of a soccer stadium in the middle of the jungle

In Manaus, takes off his clothes and plunges
Into the moonlit river only to become the fish

Who forgot the upstream way home. Lester who
Is dying and who's become the ticking in my clock.

Harry Dean says Rebecca De Mornay broke
His heart. Now Lester has mine in his mouth

And when he yawns, you can see the black moths
Stuck to the cavernous palate. Who will save

Harry Dean from dying? Who will save Lester
From erasure and the fact that only my daughter

And I (now) will speak his name out of the shadows.
Come, Lester, the sun is dying, but not so soon.

Look out the window at the silvering river and
    the man
Swimming upstream who glistens and shimmers

And takes his next deep breath, don't stop singing.

ODE TO THELMA RITTER

There's no one like you in the movies
anymore, Thelma, no lovable, middle-aged
character actress, gravelly voiced and
hard-boiled, with a sharp-tongued flair
for the cynical as well as the comical. You
could work miracles with a little screen time,
turning out indelible performances in a matter
of minutes: Bette Davis's acerbic sidekick
in *All About Eve*, Jimmy Stewart's down-to-
earth nurse in *Rear Window*, Doris Day's
perpetually hung-over maid in *Pillow Talk*.
You played women with names like Clancy,
Aggie, Bertha, Birdie, Lottie, Leena, Della,
Stella, Sophie, Sadie, Maude, Mae, and Moe.
But what of you, Thelma? Online I find only
this mini-biography. Born in Brooklyn on
Valentine's Day in 1905. Trained at American
Academy of Dramatic Arts. Stage career
mostly unsuccessful. Married Joseph Moran
in 1927; briefly gave up acting to raise two children.
Started working again in radio in
1940. Bit part in *Miracle on 34th Street* launched
noteworthy screen career. Appeared in thirty
films between 1947 and 1968. Died of a heart
attack in 1969 in New York. Thelma, six times

you were nominated for Best Supporting
Actress, and six times you lost. You, who
could save any movie with your wisecracks!
A Google search uncovers this little-known fact:
"Shirley Booth was not the first choice to play
Hazel. Thelma Ritter was. Miss Ritter wanted
the role badly, but due to illness had to bow out."
Booth would win two Emmys in the early '60s
for playing television's sassiest maid – your
rightful part. O elusive trophies! O tired heart!
You, who survived the Titanic in one picture,
would say sadly, world-wearily, in the next:
"I have to go on making a living so I can die."

ELISHA COOK, JR.
1903–1995

"We've got to have a fall guy." – Sam Spade

He's our kneecapped sap, punk chump
left holding humiliation's leaky bag,
the pouting patsy whose gat slips
his grip, hare-eyed gunsel who always

craps out at fortune's crooked table.
"Keep riding me, and they're gonna
be picking iron out of your liver,"
he warns Spade in *The Maltese Falcon*,

only to get trussed up with his own coat.
"You're a low-down lyin' Yankee," he calls
hired-gun Wilson in *Shane*, then draws
way too late. "If a guy's playin'

a hand, I let him play it," he, the stoolie,
says to Marlowe in *The Big Sleep*, before he's
forced to chug a toxic cocktail and spills
some cocked-up skinny. It's good

to see him stalk into quicksand or catch
a hot grenade, with his unstitched twitch,
his shifty-lipped little why-me routine,
this twerpy jerk who takes the rap for us.

BAD MOVIE, BAD AUDIENCE

Matinees are the best time
for bad movies – squad cars
spewing orange flame, the telephone

dead in the babysitter's hand.
Glinting with knives and missiles,

men stalk through the double
wilderness of sex and war

all through the eerie
fictions of the afternoon.
The audience is restless,

a wicked ocean roughing up its boats.

It makes a noise I seem to need.
The ruby bracelet

clinks against the handcuff,
all the cars make squealing sounds.
The kid in front of me

wants more candy,
rocks in her velvet seat. *Shut up,*

says her mother, maybe seventeen.
Just shut the fuck up.

The corpses of the future
drift across the galaxy with nothing
in their stiff, irradiated hands.

In our ears the turbo revs,
the cheekbone cracks,
a stocking slithers to the floor.

Cocteau said film is death at work.

Out of the twilight
a small voice hisses

Shut up, just shut the fuck up.

LOVE LETTER TO PAM GRIER

Dearest Pam,
I still dream of you.
College. Our second date.
How the ceiling fan would not cure
my fever that day, the white walls
beaded in sweat. I could have killed
my white friend for walking in on us.
Or kissed him right there in the dorms.
Damn the smoldering Newport cherry
that bathed my room in red. And you
cocking back that cold, hard Glock
against Samuel L. Jackson's dick.
My white friend and I, we could have
unzipped in front of the TV screen
and wrestled for the tube of Lubriderm.
I don't know what scared me more:
my roommate's wood or the camera,
out of breath, climbing mountains –
those muscled, brown thighs.
How were we supposed to compete
with Sam? Richard Pryor! Or Kareem?
With any man on your list of lays?
My mother's answer: *fuck foreplay* –
the other Pam's bed-tanned *Baywatch*
castmates taped to her teen son's wall.

For my thirteenth birthday she framed you
garnishing a large bed in red lingerie.
I'm sorry. I never hung your poster.
Even now I don't know how
to love you right. But I suspect I was
onto something back in middle school,
unsticking the other Pam
to make room for my present –
four walls. So blank
and unassuming.

128 MARCUS WICKER (1984–)

AUTEURS

BRESSON'S MOVIES

A movie of Robert
Bresson's showed a yacht,
at evening on the Seine,
all its lights on, watched

by two young, seemingly
poor people, on a bridge adjacent,
the classic boy and girl
of the story, any one

one cares to tell. So
years pass, of course, but
I identified with the young,
embittered Frenchman,

knew his almost complacent
anguish and the distance
he felt from his girl.
Yet another film

of Bresson's has the
aging Lancelot with his
awkward armor standing
in a woods of small trees,

dazed, bleeding, both he
and his horse are,
trying to get back to
the castle, itself of

no great size. It
moved me, that
life was after all
like that. You are

in love. You stand
in the woods, with
a horse, bleeding.
The story is true.

INGMAR BERGMAN'S *SEVENTH SEAL*

This is the way it is. We see
three ages in one: the child Jesus
innocent of Jerusalem and Rome
– magically at home in joy –
that's the year from which
our inner persistence has its force.

The second, Bergman shows us,
carries forward image after image
of anguish, of the Christ crossd
and sends up from open sores of the plague
(shown as wounds upon His corpse)
from lacerations in the course of love
(the crown of whose kingdom tears the flesh)

... There is so much suffering!
What possibly protects us
from the emptiness, the forsaken cry,
the utter dependence, the vertigo?
Why do so many come to love's edge
only to be stranded there?

The second face of Christ, his
evil, his Other, emaciated, pain and sin.

Christ, what a contagion!
What a stink it spreads round

our age! It's our age!
and the rage of the storm is abroad.
The malignant stupidity of statesmen rules.
The old riders thru the forests race
    shouting: the wind! the wind!
Now the black horror cometh again.

And I'll throw myself down
as the clown does in Bergman's *Seventh Seal*
to cower as if asleep with his wife and child,
hid in the caravan under the storm.

Let the Angel of Wrath pass over.
Let the end come.
War, stupidity and fear are powerful.
We are only children. To bed! to bed!
    To play safe!

To throw ourselves down
helplessly, into happiness,
    into an age of our own, into
    our own days.
There where the Pestilence roars,
where the empty riders of the horror go.

134 ROBERT DUNCAN (1919–88)

AFTER RIEFENSTAHL

The screen's fabrications remain. A film
shot never fails, sailing through the century
like a black V at the hour of moaning.
I premiere these pontifical birds: villagers march
and raise their arms, *Marschlieder*. Thus I am
your sweet messenger glittering more than first stars,
a harvest of light concealing your nicks and little
    deaths.
My comrade, my camera, my power, my fury,
my triumph, my will: do you not also,
my love, flicker in a cathedral of terror?

IN DE SICA'S *BICYCLE THIEF*

In de Sica's *The Bicycle Thief*
all Italy takes refuge
under roof eaves
waiting for the rain to stop,
and its 0 0 0 0 0's
become halos,
multiplication of wheels
reflected on the pavement.
The sidewalk's other side
singled out by passing sun beams,
not for you.

You would like to pause,
put space in the search
and the sign-up days
at the Monte Dí Pietá pawn shop –
each step more seeking than finding,
you are so tired with seeing.

Bruno, you are just a child,
follow a lank man
and don't dare cry
or touch his coatsleeve
with your hand –
grey and stubbled

like the hobo's face
before his free Sunday shave.
Will you walk home?
The rails touch where you'll never reach,
you try to think what crime
you've been condemned to.

SCRIPT MEETING

So, there's this guy – what is he, forty, fifty?
He has a condition, a history. Exurban, depressed,
      but alert,
his senses are sharp.
He hears the little hiccups embedded in the pattern
      of sound.
Sleep-walking in the woods,
premonitions of cataclysms,
flashbacks to black ops –
all of which you do a nice job of establishing under the
      opening credits –
dimple, we might say, the emptiness of his days.
And, then, next, cue the family memories:
the accident on I-5,
the eighteen-wheeler, rain, fog, a doe;
the lake, the stalled outboard motor, the rogue wave;
the explosion in the warehouse,
which is very good,
something needs to be blown up right about here.
But we have to know what actually happened sooner
rather than later. Remember,
our reputation as a studio is built not on suspense
but on horror.
We like the genetically engineered second wife
      and son.

The zombie in the basement, not so much.
Only a little bit less tedious than
his guilt-soaked diary entries in a fine copperplate
        hand
are the drooling flashes of nobility interspersing his
        psychotic episodes.
You have his eyeballs
twitching out of their sockets right here,
and how many times have we seen that before, how
        many times
have we left the multiplex disappointed,
convinced our needs will never be satisfied by
the world's mimetic gestures?
Don't leave us feeling like that. Stick with your guy.
He's his own zombie.
He haunts his own nights.
Not in this life will he tear himself from the bank of
        the burning river,
hotfooting it on the radiating marl
as his arrow of longing seeks the other shore.
Not in this life, or the next. Show us
what that means to him and what he means to it.
As our master said so long ago
in the London drawing room brilliant with
        candelabras,

139

"Here let us linger as the coal-fired Victorian
          ambience
curses outside.
Never forget that both in art and that which art
          comprehends
the whom you create is the key,
it is to the whom you create that the what,
after all so trivial, so adventitious, upon examination,
will, or, as likely, will not, happen.
The rest we can manage digitally."

From *THE FACE*

XXXVI.

I grew up in Peckinpah's valley, the brutal San
      Joaquin,
& I suppose at last I think I may belong here after all,
      in the West,
Its deserts driving my Symbolist sensibilities to
      blossom like the raw
Silk at the tips of the saguaro. When Peckinpah left for
      Los Angeles,
His crew of local theater folks followed, too, including
      my mother,
To find their futures in another, more southern
Desert land, which held its own peculiar light, that
      light ratcheting
In the shaking frames of film. My mother came home,
      but Sam pushed on,
& the world continued to burn. "Rage flares, if always
      in the heart. . . ." That
Austere angelic resonance of the West's love of power,
      grace, & violence.
I look at my friends – at Larry, Jimi the Lion, Lance, &
      Frank – all of us
Carrying in some way the marks & scars of that valley.
      (*Oh God, I'm sorry,*

I'm so, so sorry ... That's what I heard someone say one
    night, drunk & alone.)
All of that self-hatred purified most elegantly in that
    refining fire. (*I'm sorry,*
Oh God, I'm so, so sorry. ...) So, I think of Peckinpah's
    legacy echoing still
Along the bones of these sorry sons – every last one of
    us, forever after,
Just ... Peck's boys. ...

LAST TANGO

It is disquieting, that film
In which the plagued protagonist
Won't tell his lover who he is.
It's not just that she turns on him
Or that his youth and age consist
Primarily of chances missed:
The most disturbing thing's that he,
Who loses all else, cannot lose
His own identity.

All life conspires to define us,
Weighing us down with who we are,
Too much drab pain. It is enough
To make one take sides with Plotinus:
Sweet Universal Avatar,
Make me pure spirit, an ensouled star –
Or something slightly less divine:
Rain on an awning, or wind rough
Among clothes on a line.

Of course, it wouldn't do to flee
All longings, griefs, despairs, and such.
Blisses anonymously pursued
Destroy us or, evasively,
Both yield to and resist our touch.

The Brando figure learns as much:
A wholly personal collapse
Succeeds his nameless interlude.
One thinks, though, that perhaps

In some less fallen world, an ease
Might grace our necessary fictions.
There, our identities would be
Like – what? – like Haydn's symphonies,
Structures of balanced contradictions,
For all their evident restrictions,
Crazy with lightness and desire:
La Passione, Mercury,
Tempesta, Mourning, Fire.

ORSON

Orson Welles has been my philosopher
for the last few weeks now and if he's just a
phenomenon and doesn't really have a system
as Spinoza did or Anaxagoras, he
at least is consistent even if some of the things
he talks about are immensely unimportant
except to actors maybe or gossipmongers.

It was 1950 – I think – in a Protestant church
near the Pont d'Austerlitz we met him directing
a small troupe in *Macbeth* even before he
made the movie; he was taking a vacation
from America during the naming of names and I had
the honor not only of watching them rehearse
but having some *vin ordinaire* afterwards.

Of the poets, it was Dylan Thomas he seemed to
love the most and just because I could speak
one poem after another he assumed
I was a tub-thumper myself though it was Stevens –
an English edition – and Hopkins I carried around
and hateful Pound I dragged from place to place
and Crane, his ecstasy.

As far as God
Orson, like every secularist, was evasive
and spoke of unknown gases and random objects
floating through the universe and called what was
        called
sin just selfishness – this from a heavyweight
eating his steaks and potatoes at 2 or 3 a.m.
the No. 1 saint of the sinners of old Hollywood.

STALKER

There's a decided lack of flowers in The Zone.
Weeds, sure. And mud. There are no lime-tree bowers
  in The Zone.

There's a feral dog and lots of poisonous water.
There's three Russians traveling literally for hours in
    The Zone –

two guys and a close-shorn Stalker (not much of a
    talker,
that one), on the hunt for mystical powers in The
    Zone,

whatever those might be. One guy's a writer and super
    ponderous;
the other's an earnest prof. Why are there no whisky
  sours in The Zone?

That might liven things up a bit, provide some levity.
As it is, one guy sits brooding, as another cowers in
    The Zone,

curled up like a fetal pig, surrounded by the detritus of
    a lost world:
ruined dachas and smashed up towers in The Zone.

These guys are really filthy, too, and must reek to
      high heaven.
Is there a law against taking showers in The Zone?

Now someone's gone and made a video game of the
      film.
There's guns and monsters that the "meatgrinder"
      devours in The Zone.

And Chernobyl's in the subtitle for pop-toxic effect,
as Andrei's psychic child, gone before me, lowers in
      The Zone.

FLASHBACKS

SCARY MOVIES

Today the cloud shapes are terrifying,
and I keep expecting some enormous
black-and-white B-movie Cyclops
to appear at the edge of the horizon,

to come striding over the ocean
and drag me from my kitchen
to the deep cave that flickered
into my young brain one Saturday

at the Baronet Theater where I sat helpless
between my older brothers, pumped up
on candy and horror – that cave,
the litter of human bones

gnawed on and flung toward the entrance,
I can smell their stench as clearly
as the bacon fat from breakfast. This
is how it feels to lose it –

not sanity, I mean, but whatever it is
that helps you get up in the morning
and actually leave the house
on those days when it seems like death

in his brown uniform
is cruising his panel truck
of packages through your neighborhood.
I think of a friend's voice

on her answering machine –
Hi, I'm not here –
the morning of her funeral,
the calls filling up the tape

and the mail still arriving,
and I feel as afraid as I was
after all those vampire movies
when I'd come home and lie awake

all night, rigid in my bed,
unable to get up
even to pee because the undead
were waiting underneath it;

if I so much as stuck a bare
foot out there in the unprotected air
they'd grab me by the ankle and pull me
under. And my parents said there was

nothing there, when I was older
I would know better, and now
they're dead, and I'm older,
and I know better.

EARLY CINEMA

According to Mister Hedges, the custodian
who called upon their parents
after young Otwiner and young Julia
were spotted at the matinee
of Rudolph Valentino in *The Sheik*
at the segregated Knickerbocker Theater
in the uncommon Washington December
of 1922, "Your young ladies
were misrepresenting themselves today,"
meaning, of course, that they were passing.
After coffee and no cake were finished
and Mister Hedges had buttoned his coat
against the strange evening chill,
choice words were had with Otwiner and Julia,
shame upon the family, shame upon the race.

How they'd longed to see Rudolph Valentino,
who was swarthy like a Negro, like the finest
    Negro man.
In *The Sheik*, they'd heard, he was turbaned,
whisked damsels away in a desert cloud.
They'd heard this from Lucille and Ella
who'd put on their fine frocks and French,
claiming to be "of foreign extraction"
to sneak into the Knickerbocker Theater

past the usher who knew their parents
but did not know them.
They'd heard this from Mignon and Doris
who'd painted carmine bindis on their foreheads
braided their black hair tight down the back,
and huffed, "We'll have to take this up with the
    Embassy"
to the squinting ticket taker.
Otwiner and Julia were tired of Oscar Michaux,
tired of church, tired of responsibility,
rectitude, posture, grooming, modulation,
tired of homilies each way they turned,
tired of colored right and wrong.
They wanted to be whisked away.

The morning after Mister Hedges' visit
the paperboy cried "Extra!" and Papas
shrugged camel's hair topcoats over pressed pajamas,
and Mamas read aloud at the breakfast table,
"No Colored Killed When Roof Caves In"
at the Knickerbocker Theater
at the evening show
from a surfeit of snow on the roof.
One hundred others dead.

It appeared that God had spoken.
There was no school that day,
no movies for months after.

MRS MYRTLE TATE,
MOVIE PROJECTIONIST

Mrs Myrtle Tate, movie projectionist
died Wednesday in San Francisco.
    She was 66, retired.

We must remember again the absolute
excitement of the moon and think lyrically
    about her death.

It is very important for our Twentieth Century
souls because she was "one of the few women
    who worked as a movie projectionist."

Oh, honor this mothersisterbride
of magic lanterns with an endless waterfall of
    visions.

RICHARD BRAUTIGAN (1935–84)   157

SILENT FILM, DVD

Doors opened and shut,
the director shouted orders
through a bullhorn,
or babbled just

                out of the frame.
A carpenter hammered flats nearby
for the next production.
All of this, and more,
while the actors blocked it out,
already living
in that small square of light
where silence reigned
like a tiny theatre for the deaf.

Now, almost a century later,
it's peaceful, far
from the center of action,
the last voice on the street
reduced to a whisper,

                then gone.
Not even birdsong
as evening's opening credits
begin to roll.

Only the film,
shimmering out of a disc
thinner than sound,
characters moving
like fish in their gray element –
less than fish –
not a hiss, not a bubble,
not even a cry
from that dim world of silence
doubled by time.

EASY RIDER

1969, ten years old

When tree sunlight is breaking overhead, they rode

chopper bikes running the cross-country blacktops
    from
the crosshairs
  of home, not *scissor-happy* he said. Saturday is
    reaching into Sunday

like a heat argument, like your hand in the "redneck"
    neighbor's head game

        when no one is looking, or like the freedom-

need to see a painting still wet between a girl's legs in
    a field of music.

I don't have to

ask for my own freedom but I am

      willing to ask

for another's and let it hurt, marry Peter Fonda in this
    future.

Looking down

    on my own road, paved fast-black and unconsoling,
        I want

something I cannot yet name. But there are men like
        these men and my brother

            who take the sky with them when they sleep,
            when they take drugs.

There are women as I will be, adding up like matches

                between the teeth, working
on first loneliness who watch . . .

then the man in the scout truck who feels threatened,
        shotgun
aimed
at the boy-man who already stole the wind

from him.

ELENA KARINA BYRNE (1959–)   161

ATOMIC FIELD, 1972 #6

Occasionally a passerby will tramp past the basement
    window,
only his slush-covered boots visible from the
    disordered room
where she moves back and forth from the sink to the
    stove,
one strap of her red slip down around her elbow
and her red hair wild, stirring a pot,
preparing a meal for the bearded man naked
under a quilt dotted with cigarette burns
on a sofa with no legs, Daffy Duck on the portable
television inches from his sleeping face, talking
his way out of a jam with a scowling bulldog-headed
    policeman,
and nailed to the wall over the mattress in the corner
a technicolor poster of a windswept shipwrecked
    couple,
beautiful in their rags, in a movie called *Island of the
    Doomed.*

WATCHING *LAST YEAR AT MARIENBAD* AT ROGER HAGGERTY'S HOUSE IN AUBURN, ALABAMA

There is a corridor of light
through the pines, lint from the Spanish Moss.
There is the fallen sun
like ice and the twit of hidden birds
in our common backyards,
snakes threading the needles.

I walk the block past
Krogers with its exhausted wives
hovering over bins of frozen pork.

No one else has shown but their chairs are here.

We sit flanking the projector.
The opening sequence reminds Roger's
three-year-old daughter
of the wedding cake she ate last week.
It reminds me of my first train in Europe,
the windows, soft implosions
at the entrance of tunnels,
air carving its intricate laces. ...

The child has fallen asleep with a doll
on the sagging couch.

RITA DOVE (1952–)   163

AT THE MOVIES WITH MY MOTHER

Once again my mother and I have snuck out
to a movie theater, leaving behind my siblings
bruising themselves like ill-carted fruits on
a long journey and my father who remains

to be seen. In the dark and hush, we sit with
our hands greasy with the oil, sea salt and garlic
of our fried peanuts while the flickering screen
casts larger lives animated by distant puppeteers.

We're stowaways aboard a ship, I'd fantasize
of our secret excursion (perhaps not so secret).
Or Pinocchio, in search of his kind father, finds
him in the belly of Monstro the Whale. Rarely

do we watch a film I wanted. My mother favors
tearjerkers in which women suffer in martyrdom,
fall from high grace, seek revenge, and reap moral
redemption. In this communal, cavernous space

celluloid glow outlines each solitary audience,
embraced by air-conditioning, drowsing into
forgetfulness. I see my mother's eyes are fires
that could burn the unearthly core of a whale.

164 JOSEPH O. LEGASPI (1971–)

MY MOTHER AND CLARK GABLE ON THE
WORLD'S MOST FAMOUS BEACH

The racy Atlantic pounds behind them
as it has been paid to, the sun flatters
the back of her knee. He is everything
an idol should be – tall, slick, ironic,

and fake. Behind his broad right shoulder
a strut protrudes like a clipped wing,
illogical details darken his charm,
his body tilts stiffly into my mother,

who doesn't seem to notice. She drapes
a slim arm around his neck, her fingertips
tease his collar-hairs, her other hand
straightens the crisp Windsor of his tie,

her body casts its indelible shadow
of desire his entire cardboard length.
One windblown hair tickles his mustache.
Clark smiles, she smiles, the famous

Daytona sun cackles overhead, the pier
in the background chuckles to itself
as it stabs Gable in his false back
like a jealous ex-lover, hers or his.

MICHAEL McFEE (1954–)   165

WATCHING *TESS* IN ROMANIA, 1986

Dictators Nicolae and Elena Ceaușescu ruled
Romania for twenty-five years until their execu-
tion in December 1989.

The close-up hints lips will unseal.
Will *it* drift toward or will *she*?

Her neck inches forward
as if nudged by breeze. Lips part,

the quiver so intense the camera misses it.
Eyes follow Polanski's long shot

but I cling to the strawberry
suspended a wisp away from Kinski's lips.

Quick as a striking match, Alec's fingers snip
the stem, lob the raw red forth.

She tears flesh apart, the fragrance amped
by the flame of her tongue.

I trap the heat between my ribs,
harness it to daydreams. I char

the secret files that chart our most intimate
routines, singe the tongue of the headmistress

who shames me for red-staining my lips.
When classmates leap off rooftops,

I cleave to that strawberry,
each seed a narrative of dissent.

THE WEEPIES

Most Saturday afternoons
At the local Hippodrome
Saw the Pathe-News rooster,
Then the recurring dream

Of a lonesome drifter
Through uninterrupted range.
Will Hunter, so gifted
He could peel an orange

In a single, fluent gesture,
Was the leader of our gang.
The curtain rose this afternoon
On a lion, not a gong.

When the crippled girl
Who wanted to be a dancer
Met the married man
Who was dying of cancer,

Our hankies unfurled
Like flags of surrender.
I believe something fell asunder
In even Will Hunter's hands.

168 PAUL MULDOON (1951-)

UNSENT LETTER 4

LAST TAKE

I watch them killing my husband.
   Trained assassins, pumping round after
round from behind a camouflage truck:
   they crouch toward his crumpling form.

Under the white floodlights,
   blood jets sputter from his chest,
his head's thrown back. He shouts out a name, sliding
     down
   the white wall against the damp flag of his shadow.

A little guillotine shuts. Hands sponge the wall.
   He stands, alive again, so there's no
reason to fear this rehearsed fall, his captured cry,
   the badly cast revolution that asked his life.

The damask roses painted on the folding parlor
     screens
   of the phony embassy are real in a way, but the
     walls

are fake, and fake, too, the passion of these two naked
          human bodies
     embracing on the Aubusson: nevertheless, they
          obsess

the eye like any caress. Off-camera, the actor stroking
          his stubble
     of beard, the actress's hands on her own small
          breasts.
Presented with the mirror of our sentiments, it seems
     possible to believe that we love the world,
          ourselves –

Waiting in the wings like extras, full of desire
     projected away from us. These sky-high fingers
of light imply, off hand, all night we stand in for God
          here.
     There is nothing to fear, he gets up and falls down
          again

in slow motion. A boom swings into the frame,
     then out. Loaded dice are shaken onto green felt
          before
the trembling hands of the unwitting victims. A
          roulette
     wheel turns: the red, the black, chemin de fer.

The train crosses the border: inside, rows of people
    jammed
  together, watch, weep. Like Art featuring Life, the
    real
sky behind the starry backdrop fills with stars. The
    lovers kiss.
  I want to cry out How much? How much do you
    love each

other? But the director in his cherry-picker signals
    another take:
  The sky grows light. It's late.

NEWSREEL

It was like being in the crosshairs of a magnifying
    glass
Or the beams of the planets concentrating in a death
    ray
Passing right through me, boring a hole between

My shoes through the concrete floor all the way
To the far side of the earth. Yet it was only
Not knowing how to get where I was going,

I'd gotten lost in the parking lot on the way
To the cinder block bunker where my mother
Worked the snackbar, my father the projector.

The drive-in movie screen stretched horizon
To horizon, the whole of Texas sprawled around,
Cathedral-like De Sotos and great-finned Pontiacs

Flickering and sinister in torrents of light flooding
Down the screen. Frozen in that light, I
Might have been the disconsolate ageless

Stone-eyed child ornamenting a pillar
In a dead Roman city high up on a desert plateau.
I wasn't even as tall as the speakers mumbling

On and on the way now in my dream of extreme
Old age I hear voices mumbling interminably ...
Where does it shimmer, my refuge, grotto of my
        swimming pool

Lapping in the infinite leisure of the newsreel?
At last my mother appeared from among the cars
And led me back to the snackbar but I still hovered

Out there, turned loose among the shadows'
Disembodied passions striving for mastery
Above the tensed windshields: There gleams

Marilyn Monroe movie star enjoying her fame
In the voluptuous, eternal, present tense
Of celebrity being worked over by hands

Of her masseur. Bougainvillea overgrows
Her beach bungalow retreat of peace and pleasure,
The screen nothing now but layer on layer

Of flesh the fingers knead in a delirious ballet
Pushing, pulling, palms slippery and quick,
Ambiguous instruments of comfort or of pain.

The rush of blood to her face clouds into
White light as film stock jerks across
A void half coma blackout, half nightmare aura:

The film jammed, raw light pulsing like a bandage
On a face wrapped round and round in surgical gauze.
Wherever that light took me looms far from candy bars

And gum wrappers blazing under glass. The movie
        poster
Death ray stopped the earth revolving, time had
        stopped,
My mother's black slacks and my father's not yet
        grown goatee,

My own hands shaking nervously about were silently
        dissolving
In that ray bombarding from beyond the galaxy
Being invaded by screeching, beseeching noises

Of alien beings searching for a planetary home.
Then, up there, on the screen, frenetic in the light,
Was a hair trembling between two cloven lobes

Of shadow that were part of the projector's
Overheating brain, its brilliantly babbling, delusional,
Possessed by shadows, dispossessed brain.

174 TOM SLEIGH (1953–)

MUTOSCOPE

Swirl and smash of waves against the legs
and crossgirders of the pier, I have come to Brighton,
come as the fathers of our fathers came,
to see the past's Peep Show.
On two good legs, on one, they came,
veterans and stay-at-homes of the Great War,
all casualties, to stroll the West Pier's promenade,
past bands, flags, and minstrel shows,
past Gladys Pawsey in a high-necked bathing
        costume
riding her bicycle off the high board,
past Hokey-Pokey and Electric Shocker,
to the old Penny Palace, pennies burning hotly
in their hands, the worn watery profile
of Queen Victoria looking away from it all.
I bend to the mutoscope's lit window
to see "What the Butler Saw": a woman artlessly
taking off her clothes in a jerky striptease
I can slow down or speed up
by turning the handle of the mutoscope.
Easily I raise her from darkness –
the eye eternally aroused by what it can't touch –
to watch her brief repeating performance
that counts for so little. Or so much.
I can't be sure which.

Abruptly, *THE END* shuts down the image, but her
    story
continues as she reverses time's tawdry sequence
to dress and quickly disappear
down a maze of narrow streets and alleys
filled with the ghostly bodies and bodiless ghosts
of causality, the unredeemed and never-to-be-born
bearing her along to a flight
of shabby stairs, a rented room where she is free
as anyone to dream her dreams and smoke a cigarette,
smoke from the lit tip spiraling
in patternless patterns toward the room's bare light
    bulb,
the light I see her by harsh, violently
unforgiving, as she makes tomorrow into a question
of either/or: to leave this room, this vacancy
forever, or go on exactly as she has before.
Old ghost, your history is nameless and sexual,
you are your own enigma, victim
or heroine of an act of repetition that, once chosen,
will choose you for a lifetime.
I peer into the tunneled past,
so small, so faraway and fragmentary,
and yet, not unconnected to what I am now.
Dilapidation upon dilapidation, Brighton
is crumbling, fading to sepia tones,
as your unfunny burlesque continues past

your life, perhaps past mine,
the past preserved and persevering,
the sentimental past.

MOVIES IN CHILDHOOD

A nurse punctured my thigh
with three needles
in the middle of the night.
Most of the pain
was new. From the hospital
bed, I saw, too, an abandoned
teenager living behind walls
while another family
moved in. One spoke
of sunlight painted
a bedroom's wood floor
as the season turned.
Then his eye poured
through, darkened
his carved peephole
as a girl dressed.
In another, bells
attached to jacket lapels
hung still as the villain,
unblinking, practiced
picking a wallet.
Siphoned billfolds
passed between newspaper
tubes by the team,
theft which started

with an elbow, a sharp bump
on a busy city street.
In *Papillon*, McQueen
jumped from Devil's Island,
a leap that should have killed him.
He ate roaches in solitary,
the insects clicking just beyond
twitching fingertips.
How did you know
I wasn't contagious?
the leper asked, after McQueen
accepted his pipe. Puffing,
he said, I didn't. I almost
forgot my own sutures
until the needle bit
into his chest over
and over to paint
the butterfly. In the fire's
red light, a man's face
appeared to crack and melt.
A fellow prisoner ran
onto a treadle board trap:
spikes rose, tore clean
out his back
as, eyes twisting skyward,
he seemed to pray.

MICHAEL PAUL THOMAS (1966–)   179

BUDDY HOLLY WATCHING
REBEL WITHOUT A CAUSE
Lubbock, Texas, 1956

He's played hookey to see the flick again,
Though it's only showing at the Alhambra,

The run-down joint in the barrio. Spanish version,
Tawdry trashed marquee: *Rebelde Sin Causa.*

Dean staggers into Juvey, playing a credible drunk
Though his dubbed voice squeaks like Mickey Mouse.

Me llamo Jaime Stark. But Dean's trademark smirk
Obliterates the dialogue. Buddy studies every gesture,

Horn-rims sliding the bridge of his nose,
Though the smirk doesn't save that punk in the car,

Crashing to some stock-footage ocean, doesn't save
    Sal Mineo's
Benighted life. But Buddy, walking home, wants a
    trademark.

In shop-window reflections, he practices the Jim Dean
    strut.
Some of us, he thinks, will never get it right.

180 DAVID WOJAHN (1953–)

REMAKES

THE MOVIES

I would like to watch a movie tonight
in which a stranger rides into town
or where someone embarks on a long journey,

a movie with the promise of danger,
danger visited upon the citizens of the town
by the stranger who rides in,

or the danger that will befall the person
on his or her long hazardous journey –
it hardly matters to me

so long as I am not in danger,
and not much danger lies in watching
a movie, you might as well agree.

I would prefer to watch this movie at home
than walk out in the cold to a theater
and stand on line for a ticket.

I want to watch it lying down
with the bed hitched up to the television
the way they'd hitch up a stagecoach

to a team of horses
so the movie could pull me along
the crooked, dusty road of its adventures.

I would identify with the bartender
in the movie about the stranger
who rides into town,

the fellow who pours him his first drink
and who knows how to duck
when a chair shatters the big mirror over the bar

Or I could side with the stationmaster
in the movie about the long perilous journey,
the fellow who fishes a gold watch from his pocket,

helps a lady onto the train,
and hands up a heavy satchel
to the man with the mustache

and the dangerous eyes,
waving the all-clear to the engineer.
Then the movie would continue without me,

and at the end of the day
I would hang up my oval hat on a hook
and walk the road home to my two dogs,

my faithful, amorous wife,
and my children –
Molly, Lucinda, and Harold Jr.

SURVEY: FRANKENSTEIN UNDER THE FRONT PORCH LIGHT

I'm from the era when "special effects" was a guy
in a rubber monster costume: sometimes
in a cheapo, shoddy, barely plotted movie
you could snatch a glimpse of zipper and where
the alien skin rucked up on the actor's shins, though
that example does disservice to the Creature
from the Black Lagoon, who went through nearly 80
changes of shape at the hands of designer Milicent
   Patrick,
adding up to 18,000 of Universal-International's
   doled out
1954 dollars. Over *200* pounds of foam rubber were
   used – expenditure
unnecessary for Riva Schmitz, the mother who,
with thorned switch and a simple lock
on her daughter's sour bedroom closet, posited
– to the courts, of course, but also and repeatedly
in the dreams of every child on my block – a brutal
monsterdom enough. I remember a doggie bowl
of water was involved, and also hat pins. By our later
Alien/Avatar era, megabeasts are micropixeled
– no one rolls the pea-green Martian latex legs on
   anymore
and superglues the Styrofoam excrescences – and yet

when the-thing-like-a-fisted-arm-with-shark-teeth
punches out of the spaceman's chest (i.e.,
it hatches in its host) the lesson
is much the same as ancient Greek mythology's
(Cronus, who devoured his own children; or the
     Furies,
Those Who Walk in Darkness: writhing snakes for
     hair,
and tears of blood: "as long as sin remains in the world
they cannot be banished") ... *we're* the source of the
     horror.
Even Peggy Rabb, the sweetest poet I ever knew,
had a monster inside. So many kinds of this
one thing! Of Leviathan: "His teeth are terrible round
     about.
His scales are his pride. Out of his mouth go burning
     lamps,
out of his nostrils goeth smoke, he esteemeth iron
as straw." In Roger Corman's *Viking Women*
and the Sea Serpent, the laughable latter is a hand-
     puppet
fashioned of *papier maché*. Who would win the battle:
the wingéd elephant of the Hindus, or the wingéd
     bull

of the Babylonians? Burr-Woman "climbs upon the
    hero's back
and can't be dislodged, until he dies of fatigue."
King Kong's armatured model was only eighteen
    inches tall
(sponge, lambskin, rubber). Fire-Moccasins sets
    everything on flame
with his eponymous footwear. Gorgon. Medusa.
Yeti. Nessie. In Rilke the angels seem equally
horrific. *Even Peggy Rabb, the sweetest poet I ever knew,
had a monster inside – although she, herself,
was its victim.* It took twenty years for Emmy
– Riva Schmitz's daughter – to be arrested on charges
of child abuse, but it happened: inevitably a version of
    Burr-Woman
had been seeded in her, in her mind, in her heart,
and couldn't be dislodged. In 1956's sci-fi flick
    Forbidden Planet
the monster is an aggressively energy-crackling
    emanation
of the human id. *Yes, even Peggy Rabb.* The last time
    I visited
she was fed by tubes in her arms and through her
    nose,
and a five-year-old child who happened to pass her
    room door
screamed: a very low moment. On October 31, 1794

the optimistic British scientist Thomas Beddoes
        wrote,
"There is the best reason to hope that Cancer,
the most dreadful of human maladies, may be
        disarmed
of its terror and its danger too." *October 31. . . .*
Here they are, in the mist,
with their fists at the doors of our neighborhoods,
wearing our insides, out.

THE CONTINUITY SCRIPT: *RASHOMON*

The dazzling light of the sun breaks through the
    branches of trees overhead –
WOODCUTTER *I want . . . I will belong to whoever*
    kills the other.
as the camera travels through a dense woods.

And then I fainted. When I opened my eye and looked
    around,
I saw here, in my husband's chest, the dagger.
The dazzling light of the sun breaks through the
    branches of trees overhead –

If you are my husband then why don't you kill this man?
    Then you can tell me
to kill myself. That is what a real man would do. But you
    aren't a real man.
as the camera travels through a dense woods.

WOMAN (CONT'D) *Kill him – kill him!*
LONG SHOT of the medium in the prison courtyard,
    the wind howling about her!
The dazzling light of the sun breaks through the
    branches of trees overhead –

SAMURAI-MEDIUM *I still hear those words!*
The medium writhes in circles on her knees.
The dazzling light of the sun breaks through the
      branches of trees overhead
as the camera travels through a dense woods. Music
      begins –

OLD FRANKENSTEIN

The old man never calls.
He quit making us
settled down with his bride
in a stone cottage
went back to his smoking jacket
wrote a book and tore it up
they say, I never saw it.

I learned to talk again
in spite of them all
every crowd and Burgomaster
– read by fires, by lakes
ate what I ran across
but killed no people
not for a long time now.

The flesh has not decayed, probably can't.
I carry a cane and that explains the walk.
I dress like a cheap old man
a man with peculiarities
a man you'd leave alone
to live in a shed in the woods.
He'll die, I won't.

He can't live forever
and he doesn't like it when I show up.
I haven't tried that in twenty years.
I accumulate birthdays like everyone else.
He could call. His wife
could call. My only family.
I wonder how it will be without him.

BRUCE F. KAWIN (1945–)

BOLLYWOOD CONFABULATION
(a collage poem of famous lines translated from
Bollywood movies: *Pakeezah, Sholay, Mughal-e-Azam, Sahib Bibi Aur Ghulam*, and *Kabhi Kabhi*)

Look at your feet, so beautiful. Do
not step on the ground, filth will smear them;

your future will fill with pricks. He with a
fearful heart, understand dead. Death will dance

on your head – lift your eyes and see. I am
its servant, thirsty from birth; you my jewels

my raiments. I redden my part, adorn
myself for my beloved, terrified

of evil-eye so with black kohl I streak
my waterline. Petals shrivel but thorns

keep sharp. Love brings ruin and ruins lives.
Your lips' tremor is morning; when you let

loose your tresses, midnight. What place has fear
if a bloom's barbs do not dread withering?

VOICE OVER
(*ghost aria for Edmond O'Brien*)

Suddenly it all started
   to fall into place. It was like being
      shaken out of a doped-up pipe dream
where everything looked like
   some crazy modern painting,
      the streets and faces twisted into the wrong ratio.
I was wide awake
   and it felt like being wide awake
      for the first time in my life,
only for me that was the same as being
   in the middle of a nightmare.
      But I felt a weird relief
even as I realized just how thoroughly I'd been had.
   I could almost convince myself
      that maybe now it was a new ball game,
maybe the tables were about to turn.
   I was finally playing with a full deck
      instead of the stack of jokers they'd handed me.
A frame-up: that's what it had been from the start,
   and I was the sap it was made to order for.
      It was a beaut, all right,
with me as the fall guy
   wrapped up neatly and tied with pink ribbons.
      They must have busted a gut laughing

while they watched me stroll into their trap.
    The trail I thought I'd tumbled to
        just on account of being such a sharpie
had been mapped out long before I turned the corner.
    It might as well have been signposted
        Suckers Enter Here, or maybe
Frame Job Next Right. I thought I'd written
    the book on frame-ups, and here I turned out
        to be the main character, Exhibit A
right in the center ring. It was a story line
    constructed by a con guy with so many angles
        he made Einstein look like a dummy.
I'd been on a losing streak since page one
    and the last chapter was death. I'd been sweet-
        talked
        straight into the slaughterhouse.
Every move I'd made
    had been strictly according to plan –
        their plan. They'd cased me so well
they knew just how I'd trip myself up.
    Me, the wise guy,
        the guy that was too smart and too tough
ever to fall for a set-up like that.
    Sure, just like Adam
        wouldn't ever have sold himself short
for a taste of homegrown apple. Just like Samson
    was too cute an operator to let himself get taken

for the price of a cheap haircut.
It was the oldest game in the world,
    played for the same old stakes,
        a dame in mink with eyes a mile deep
and a bundle of money
    that couldn't have been planted more obviously
        if they'd labeled it Please Take Me.
I'd swallowed the bait
    and now they had their hooks in so deep
        I'd have to rip myself to shreds
if I ever wanted to break free of their racket.
    And maybe that was the way it had to be.
        Maybe this was the sucker they'd choke on.
They'd cut the cards,
    now they could live with the shuffle.
        It was downright comical if you thought about it.
We were all going to have a good laugh before we
        burned.
    Say, if this is when we cash the chips
        let's do it in style.
They'd get me, all right, I was gone,
    I already knew that it was checkout time
        in the luxury-class neon hotel
where nobody ever checks back in.
    But for some customers the price is always higher
        than they want to pay. This is hell, isn't it?
Hey buddy, they tell me in these parts

the coin of the realm
    is a man's life and breath
and the spare change is his everlasting soul.
    This is when I start to feel good.
        The city dawn is barging into the side streets
and I'm starting to feel almost human again
    when I think about how it will be
        finally to call in every last IOU.

KING KONG MEETS WALLACE STEVENS

Take two photographs –
Wallace Stevens and King Kong
(Is it significant that I eat bananas as I write this?)

Stevens is portly, benign, a white brush cut
striped tie. Businessman but
for the dark thick hands, the naked brain
the thought in him.

Kong is staggering
lost in New York streets again
a spawn of annoyed cars at his toes.
The mind is nowhere.
Fingers are plastic, electric under the skin.
He's at the call of Metro-Goldwyn-Mayer.

Meanwhile W. S. in his suit
is thinking chaos is thinking fences.
In his head – the seeds of fresh pain
his exorcising,
the bellow of locked blood.

The hands drain from his jacket,
pose in the murderer's shadow.

MICHAEL ONDAATJE (1943–)   199

RED LANTERNS

> "Where the master spends the night
> that mistress gets ... the lighted lanterns."
> – Second mistress to fourth mistress in
> *Raise the Red Lantern*

I have seen black-robed men
hang the adulteress,
take her, with tied wrists, ankles,
tangled hair, choked entreaties,
across a snow-bound roof
before the household wakes.

I have wound up the gramophone,
played her voice singing,
filled my room with red light,
unbraided my hair, walked
the chambers, expecting the master,
wanting his son.

I have faked pregnancies,
abused the serving girl
(the master's favorite), revealed
secrets in the heat of drink,
refused his kisses,
the solicitude of the women.

200

In each woman's courtyard
I will raise the red lantern.

FRANKENSTEIN LOVE

I think there was a movie once
where Frankenstein fell in love with a vampire.
A small mummy at first interfered
but later provided the requisite necessary
clarifications. He can only
meet you at night. Her face
is scarred in a permanent expression
of doom, but her bolt glows whenever
she sees you. The rival for the vampire's affections
was a vaguely feminine zombie. Frankenstein
felt not very mysterious. Many different
feelings cycled below whoever's
skin she had been given. Did they even
belong to her? In the many pages
of the book of love this is only one story.
But everyone goes through it once. The main
question is, will you be the one unable
to control your temper, sewed together
as you are from the past? Or the one
who always ends up turning away in search
of another likeness?

REEL LIFE

VIOLENCE

Eerie from hung drapes, blue-velvet, dark aisles,
disturbing in the bone-deep bass echo
and speakers too big for these chambers,
the theater air quickens like blood when
a huge blast explodes from the hero's side-
arm the size of a hammer, shattering
a wall of glass over the bad guy's head.
Our neighbors have ceased chewing and keep their
breath to themselves, as the scene darkens out
into gaslights down a real, rainy lane.

Tenderness accompanies these terrors.
When the lights shift, and guns come seething,
when cars careen into crowds and bad music
slams us back with cheap force, you lay your head
against my shoulder and gaze down, or squeeze
my fist until the crushing of evil
has lifted our neighbors' hearts with a start.
Tonight twelve have died, so many been hurt
that their curdling screams have sounded like ours.
Not once have these mass killings, bloodlettings,
or this cinematic gore made us sad.
Instead, it's the hero's young partner,
his quick, lonely death an hour ago,
adding the narrative need for revenge.

And not his death, really. Rather, at home,
his wife and small child asleep with their dreams,
who never knew he died and who, now that
the movie's all over, will never be
able to tell him, *We love you, goodbye*,
except in the dreams we carry home, too.

FINAL FAREWELL

Great moment in *Blade Runner* where Roy
Batty is expiring, and talks about how everything
he's seen will die with him –
ships on fire off the shoulder of Orion
sea-beams glittering before the Tannhauser gates.

Memory is like molten gold
   burning its way through the skin
it stops there.
       There is no transfer
Nothing I have seen
will be remembered
beyond me
That merciful cleaning
of the windows of creation
will be an excellent thing
my interests notwithstanding.

But then again I've never been
   near Orion, or the Tannhauser
gates,

I've only been here.

TOM CLARK (1941–2018)   207

come home from the movies,
black girls and boys,
the picture be over and the screen
be cold as our neighborhood.
come home from the show,
don't be the show.
take off some flowers and plant them,
pick us some papers and read them,
stop making some babies and raise them.
come home from the movies
black girls and boys,
show our fathers how to walk like men,
they already know how to dance.

AT THE FILM SOCIETY

On the empty walls some of the others
project 8-millimeter versions of themselves
while in the large room with the screen
Liv Ullman touches Max von Sydow
with a lust so deepened by grief
the rest of us feel our miseries
are amateurish, some of us are even elated
to have Bergman for such a friend;
oh come over for dinner, Ingmar,
and make our loneliness exquisite.

The woman sitting next to me, overweight
and beautiful, has been crying
since I took her hand and whispered "slit
wrists, betrayal, viciousness, anything
that Ullman does make me happy."
I'm not sure why she's crying, but I know
how intimacy begins and it has,
I know that the best sex rises
like a trapped beast from our vacancies,
those openings we never knew were there
until touched. Ullman now
has offered her face to theologians
as proof there is a soul; von Sydow
is looking off to the side, afraid

to let go some bottom of himself.
Later, the woman and I will talk about this
in bed, with pleasure.

How soon the others will get tired
of themselves is always a question.
Each of us has been one of them,
waited our turn, then waited again
for the praise that didn't come
fast or true enough.
Now the discussion on Bergman begins.
Now we can give ourselves.

BLONDE BOMBSHELL

Love is boring and passé, all that old baggage,
the bloody bric-a-brac, the bad, the gothic,
retrograde, obscurantist hum and drum of it
needs to be swept away. So, night after night,
we sit in the dark of the Roxy beside grandmothers
with their shanks tied up in the tourniquets
of rolled stockings and open ourselves, like earth
to rain, to the blue fire of the movie screen
where love surrenders suddenly to gangsters
and their cuties. There in the narrow,
mote-filled finger of light, is a blonde,
so blonde, so blinding, she is a blizzard, a huge
spook, and lights up like the sun the audience
in its galoshes. She bulges like a deuce coupe.
When we see her we say good-bye to Kansas.
She is everything spare, cool, and clean,
like a gas station on a dark night and the cold
dependable light of rage coming in on schedule like
        a bus.

OLD MOVIE WITH THE SOUND
TURNED OFF

The hatcheck girl wears a gown that glows;
The cigarette girl in the black fishnet stockings
And a skirt of black, gauzy, bunched-up tulle
That bobs above the pert muffin of her bottom –
She must be twenty-two – would look like a dancer
In Degas except for the tray of cigarettes that rests
Against her – *tummy* might have been the decade's
     word,
And the thin black strap which binds it to her neck
And makes the whiteness of her skin seem swan's-
     down
White. Some quality in the film stock that they used
Made everything so shiny that the films could not
Not make the whole world look like lingerie, like
Phosphorescent milk with winking shadows in it.
All over the world the working poor put down their
     coins,
Poured into theaters on Friday nights. The manager
     raffled –
"Raffled off," we used to say in San Rafael in my
     postwar
Childhood into which the custom had persisted –
Sets of dishes in the intermission of the double
     feature –

Of the kind they called Fiestaware. And now
The gangster has come in, surrounded by an
    entourage
Of prize fighters and character actors, all in tuxedo
And black overcoats – except for him. His coat is
    camel
(Was it the material or the color? – my mind wanders
To earth-colored villages in Samara or Afghanistan).
He is also wearing a white scarf which seems to
    shimmer
As he takes it off, after he takes off the gray fedora
And hands it to the hatcheck girl. The singer,
In a gown of black taffeta that throws off light
In starbursts, wears black gloves to her elbows
And as she sings, you sense she is afraid.
Not only have I seen this film before – the singer
Shoots the gangster just when he thinks he's been
    delivered
From a nemesis involving his brother, the district
    attorney,
And a rival mob – I know the grandson of the
    cigarette girl,
Who became a screenwriter and was blackballed later
Because she raised money for the Spanish Civil War.
Or at least that's the story as I remember it, so that,
When the gangster is clutching his wounded gut
And delivering a last soundless quip and his scarf

Is still looking like the linen in Heaven, I realize
That it is for them a working day and that the dead
Will rise uncorrupted and change into flannel slacks,
Hawaiian shirts; the women will put on summer
    smocks
Made from the material superior dish towels are
    made of
Now, and they'll all drive up to Malibu for drinks.
All the dead actors were pretty in their day. Why
Am I watching this movie? you may ask. Well, my
    beloved,
Down the hall, is probably laboring over a poem
And is not to be disturbed. And look! I have
    rediscovered
The sweetness and the immortality of art. The actress
Wrote under a pseudonym, died, I think, of cancer of
    the lungs.
So many of them did. Far better for me to be doing
    this
(A last lurid patch of fog out of which the phrase
    "The End"
Comes swimming; the music I can't hear surging now
Like fate) than reading with actual attention my field
    guides
Which inform me that the flower of the incense cedar
I saw this morning by the creek is "unisexual, solitary,
    and terminal."

VARIATION ON A BLACK CINEMA TREASURE: *BROKEN EARTH*

Broken Earth
Year of Release: 1939
Running Time: 11 minutes
Cast: Clarence Muse and unidentified boy

I am the sick boy in the shack when the camera opens
On the sunrise and wispy silhouettes of the plow
And the fool mule and my father working a row down

The middle of a rock field with a small shack in one
    corner
And a shade tree in the other where a crew of barefoot

Old black men stoop and sing "All God's Chillun Wear
    Shoes"
And call out *Hey* and *Hi* and the name of my father
Who goes on plowing into sundown, into the dark
    hour

When the mule will grunt no farther and the red eyes
Of the black men's cigarettes blaze and flicker in one
    corner

Of the field as I quiver in a wet skin in the hot small
    light
Of the lantern blazing and flickering in the shack.
I am a sick boy. I am as still as a kettle of water. I am
    waiting

To be rearranged by the hand of God, which is not
    the hand
Of God, but the strip of cloth pressed against my brow

By my father who has no medicine but prayer.
I don't know what I did to get here mumbling
"Pappy" and calling out to the ghost of my mother

As a choir sings "Swing Low, Sweet Chariot"
    somewhere.
I don't know who it is telling me to open my eyes.

AFTER THE MOVIE

My friend Michael and I are walking home arguing
        about the movie.
He says that he believes a person can love someone
and still be able to murder that person.

I say, No, that's not love. That's attachment.
Michael says, No, that's love. You can love someone,
        then come to a day

when you're forced to think "it's him or me"
think "me" and kill him.

I say, Then it's not love anymore.
Michael says, It was love up to then though.

I say, Maybe we mean different things by the same
        word.
Michael says, Humans are complicated: love can exist
        even in the murderous heart.

I say that what he might mean by love is desire.
Love is not a feeling, I say. And Michael says, Then
        what is it?

We're walking along West 16th Street – a clear
     unclouded night – and I hear my voice
repeating what I used to say to my husband: Love is
     action, I used to say to him.

Simone Weil says that when you really love you are
     able to look at someone
   you want to eat and not eat them.

Janis Joplin says, take another little piece of my heart
     now baby.

Meister Eckhart says that as long as we love any
     image we are doomed to live in purgatory.

Michael and I stand on the corner of 6th Avenue
     saying goodnight.
I can't drink enough of the tangerine spritzer I've just
     bought –

again and again I bring the cold can to my mouth and
     suck the stuff from
the hole the flip top made.

What are you doing tomorrow? Michael says.
But what I think he's saying is "You are too strict. You
     are a nun."

218

Then I think, Do I love Michael enough to allow him
    to think these things of me even if he's not
    thinking them?

Above Manhattan, the moon wanes, and the sky turns
    clearer and colder.
Although the days, after the solstice, have started to
    lengthen,

we both know the winter has only begun.

MERTON, LAX AND MY FATHER

Thomas Merton and Robert Lax used to drive over to
    Bradford PA from Olean
For a night out in the bars, looking for girls, hitting
    the movie theaters –
It was 1938. Bradford was a money-jingling oil town
    then. Merton was working
On his masters thesis on Blake, not yet a monk, had
    just found that Blake had
Read the Bhagavad-Gita and the Far Eastern mystics.
    Lax, not yet self-exiled, not yet
The poet but following a holy inner lure, and any girl
    who matched his stare.
I was born in Bradford, but not for another eleven
    years. My father was driving
A truck for Bradford Laundry and taking a
    correspondence course in refrigeration.
He was that rare guy who actually finished and aced
    such chances he found
Advertised in the back pages of *Argosy* and *The
    Bradford Era*. Not yet in the Army,
Had not gone to the Pacific. Had just played his first
    game of pool and wondered
Why the preacher was so down on it. He didn't drink,
    so he wouldn't have

Run into the pair in a bar, arm wrestled with the one-
    day famous monk.
But he went to the movies. Bunches of adventure films
    hit the screen that year:
Adventure in Sahara, *Adventures of Marco Polo*. And
    Blondes at Work with
Glenda Farrell, *Bluebeard's Eighth Wife* with Claudette
    Colbert. He didn't dance
Like Merton and Lax, but he probably saw *Swing Your
    Partner* with Humphrey Bogart.
I know this is a stretch, but I imagine him in row
    seven with his arm around my
Mother, watching some silly flick like *Boys Town* with
    Spencer Tracy,
And turning around to the two clowns laughing and
    throwing popcorn and saying,
Knock it off, you guys. He had a stare that could make
    you break out in boils, but
He would have been a mere silhouette to them. *Hey
    you bozos, I said knock it off.*

TV

Going come dark so my madda call me
fo go back inside da house.
Can smell tonkatsu from da kitchen
and my madda turn on da TV.
"Dinner going be ready soon."

I watch TV, and dey playing *Superman*.
"Mommy, one day I going save everybody.
I going be Superman."
She turn da tonkatsu ova in da pan
and tell me das one good idea.

Den, get one commercial about trips to Hawai'i.
"Mommy, one day we going Hawai'i."
She look at me funny kine.
I tell her as one good idea fo go Hawai'i.
Everybody can live in grass shacks
and going be good fun fo drink da kine
tropical drink wit da fruit and umbrella
and stay outside all da time.
She tell me we live Hawai'i.

I look at her.
"No, we no live Hawai'i.
We live in one house like everybody on da TV."

She tell me one mo time we live Hawai'i
and dinner going be ready pretty soon.
My madda dunno wat she talking about.
We no live Hawai'i.

Now, da TV playing one old movie.
My madda said as *Breakfast at Tiffany's*
and da lady da actress Audrey Hepburn.
Look like one nice lady. I like her.

Get one wild party and dis guy wit small eyes
talking weird. I no undastand wat he saying.
"Mommy, who dat guy?"
My madda no answer, and she move da katsu
on one plate. She tell me dinner ready.

I eat and she tell me we going have
spaghetti tomorrow. I like spaghetti.
"So who da guy wit da small eyes in da movie?

Da one dat talk funny."
She tell me she dunno who him,
but in da movie, he suppose to be one Oriental guy.
"Yeah?"
She wen nod and tell me fo eat.

223

"Wat Oriental?"
She look surprise. "Us Oriental."
"I thought we Japanese?"
"We Japanese."

Afta she pau wash dishes,
she hold me close, and I can hear
her heart and her voice vibrate wen she talk.
Den, she stroke my hair, and I get sleepy.

My madda tink she know everyting,
but she dunno.
I not Oriental,
I no live Hawai'i,
and one day I going save everybody
just like Superman.

SUBTITLE

We present for you this evening
A movie of death: observe
These scenes chipped celluloid
Reveals unsponsored and tax-free.

We request these things only:
All gum must be placed beneath the seats
Or swallowed quickly, all popcorn sacks
Must be left in the foyer. The doors
Will remain closed throughout
The performance. Kindly consult
Your programs: observe that
There are no exits. This is
A necessary precaution.

Look for no dialogue, or for the
Sound of any human voice: we have seen fit
To synchronize this play with
Squealings of pigs, slow sound of guns,
The sharp dead click
Of empty chocolatebar machines.
We say again: there are
No exits here, no guards to bribe,
No washroom windows.

No finis to the film unless
The ending is your own.
Turn off the lights, remind
The operator of his union card:
Sit forward, let the screen reveal
Your heritage, the logic of your destiny.

UPON THE ACTOR'S LONGING FOR THE ALIENATION EFFECT

Though larger than life
the actor lived in fear and trembling
behind the literal screen,
cutting a sliver into the white square
to watch the public watching him
in the debut of his new film.
Unknowingly he looked,
at times, through his own eye,
like a painting in a haunted house
without its power of the gaze,
reactions to his acting
owning his sense of self.
If they laughed or cried on cue,
he still doubted his value,
longing to tear the screen away
and risk approval
beyond performance
of his overpaid identity.

HAJI KHAVARI (1986–)   227
TRANSLATED BY ROGER SEDARAT

HOLLYWOOD NIGHTS

When June Haver sang "Deep In The Heart of Texas,"
stars burnt bright deep in my solar plexus.
Fluff fifteen, love was a Perfect Stranger
though I kept my hair mussed up like Farley Granger.

But trenchcoat Mitchums were more my style. A fag
hung from my mouth (unlit, I'd tried one drag,
thrown up and met in the glass a watery eye
like Van Heflin's when Shane rode out to die).

I fixed a sign – RICK'S BAR – above my door
through which the dame might walk. "Je t'adore"
gloss lips would plead. But I could play it tough:
Milland's half-sneer, Wayne's shrug, Coop's stare –
        enough

to drop Blyth, Kerr or Bergman on their knees
sobbing "I was wrong to leave you, please,
just one more chance?" But no, the door would slam
and "Frankly my dears I don't give a damn"

I'd cough in blood on the keyboard as a haze
mantled my eyes. Then, the Last Polonaise!
The screen goes blank as punters mop their eyes.
Next showing: June meets Burt in A WILD SURMISE.

228 JOHN LUCAS (1937–)

A FABLE

Driving into the heart of night we arrive at the part
of the movie where I start tap-dancing, tap-tapping
across a tin sheet, a sort of surfing airborne pan

listing side to side and back and me
tilting to balance, announcing I am Esther Williams.
All is blue, salty with prayer and incantation, all

dazzling aristocratic hands. But it wasn't the heart
of night. There was no heart. It was true
about the tilting, but the movie not a movie at all,

just the usual drivel and sludge, and never having seen
Esther Williams, in truth I'd only conjured a wet
        black forties
one-piece and rubber bathing cap – which is always
        the case

when you're afraid. Oh what's the use. Why beat about
        the bush,
grief's freeze-frame churchyard with its fresh cut
        dirge,
its pretend heaven. Watch me driving myself down

a winding country road, top down, one hand on the
    wheel, the other
grabbing back my thick blond hair like some Italian
    Movie Star,
some Monica Vitti, whose leopard kerchief the wind
    sucked off

long ago – Hours? Decades? Now
wanting a bit of *chachacha*, she flips the radio dial
    loosing
a grassy static, a spasmodic numbing hive-buzz of
    stumbling bees.

She flips it off. She'll be drifting in that static soon
    enough
with her ballet flats and tin rigor mortis. *Allora!*
    In bocca a lupo
cries a child's nightlight, while night releases its
    indifferent stars.

A SERENE HEART AT THE MOVIES

She strode to her car and turned the key and
a peony of bomb bloomed all at once.
The film is rated R for violence.
Dear fellow readers of the *Iliad*,
they found half her pinkie in the roses.
Guns are the jewelry of men. And cars –
think how much the script must have hated her
to blow her up in the burgundy Rolls.
But she's not real; it's only a movie.
Those blood-drenched dreams we wake from in a
     baste
of sweat, like our sex fantasies, aren't real
to moral life. They don't impede at all
the love we make, the money, or the haste.
So hush now, little baby, don't you cry.

ABSOLUTELY EARTH

I like movies because
I get to look
at other people
it's so lonely at night
there aren't any movies
about swans
or buildings
though I saw one where a building
kept coming back
a little square red one
well actually
it was a hospital
a haunted one
kept coming around
a movie's like a solar system
three slow planets maybe four
urging toward inevitability
a plot in a car
the foot of the dead man
sticking out on a hill
and the music swells
I thought this is like
my love life
all at once I get
it and it's really too

much
you could see it coming
& then it went
the shit hit the fan
through a little
trap door
on the floor
just look at all these
people on my
screen

POISON LIGHT
For J. Overstreet

Last night
I played Kirk Douglas to
Your Burt Lancaster. Reflecting
20 years of tough guys I
Saw at the Plaza Theatre in
Buffalo, New York. I can
Roll an L like Bogart
You swagger like Wayne

Ours was a bad performance
The audience, our friends
Panned it. The box office
Hocked the producers

We must stop behaving like
The poison light we grew on

Ancient loas are stranded
They want artfare home
Our friends watch us. They
Want to hear what we say

Let's face it
My eye has come a long way
So has your tongue
They belong on a pyramid wall
Not in a slum
(*Dead End*, 1937)

LINCOLN

Hanging from the tip of Lincoln's nose,
Cary Grant had one second of the sensation
that draws the swallows to a height
where they no longer have that wing-skate
propulsion through layers but glide
like their distant cousins, the buzzards
stirring the sky between cloud and corpse.
As perspectives go, it's hard to argue
with circle and sweep, and at intervals
they let go a steely peep, the way a nickel
dropped from the Empire State Building
hits the pavement harmlessly between
taxis: one in use; the other going uptown
beyond the river, into the private streets.

MOVIE

Spotlight her face   her face has no light in it
touch the cheek with light   inform the eyes
press meanings on those lips.

                              See cities from the air,
fix a cloud in the sky, one bird in the bright air,
one perfect mechanical flower in her hair.

Make your young men ride over the mesquite plains;
produce our country on film: here are the flaming
        shrubs,
the Negroes put up their hands in Hallelujahs,
the young men balance at the penthouse door.

We focus on the screen: look   they tell us
you are a nation of similar whores   remember the
        Maine
remember you have a democracy of champagne –

And slowly the female face kisses the young man,
over his face the twelve-foot female head
the yard-long mouth enlarges and yawns
                                        The End

Here is a city   here the village grows
here are the rich men standing rows on rows,
but the crowd seeps behind the cowboy the lover the
        king,
past the constructed sets America rises
the bevelled classic doorways   the alleys of trees are
        witness
America rises in a wave a mass
pushing away the rot.

                    The Director cries Cut!
hoarsely CUT   and the people send pistons of force
crashing against the CUT! CUT! of the straw men.

Light is superfluous upon these eyes,
across our minds push new portents of strength
destroying the sets, the flat faces, the mock skies.

THE MOVIE

One day I stumbled on a movie set
Of University Place: a surreal park,
A pointillist mews with gleaming iron gates,
Shuttered buildings hollow at the back,

Streetlights that would topple in a breeze.
Leaving my house, clutching the rubbery basket
I use for farmer's-market vegetables,
Gingerly, I walked into a street

Stripped of actual traffic, to discover
"Freshmen" chattering like orioles. A man
In canvas overalls, crowd choreographer,
Barked syllables in opposite directions,

And set us off, a passersby ballet
Whose paths were planned. Some watched for non-
        existent
Green lights; one woman nervously
Darted, jostling books from pseudo-students.

Then a flower vendor wheeled a wagon
Past us. An actor ran with outstretched arms,
Missed it and cursed it, green eyes so forlorn
I knew that he would follow those geraniums

Forever. And that was all the cameras
Reeled in that morning: one scene with the same
Brightness that had possessed me over the years
I sailed with Bette Davis in a storm

Of black-and-white, trailed Bogart's enemies
Who wear magenta neckties (colorized),
And wept through *Les Enfants du paradis*.
When the director let us go, I realized

That the protection of familiar things
Was limited. At best I was a stranger.
Undoubtedly, the market would be traveling
On wheels to another city, and the copy center

Delivered elsewhere, shelves and window panes.
Some crew would sandblast the "U.S. Government
Post Office" block letters, engraved in stone.
Seeing mica glitter on the pavement,

I scrutinized my neighbors for their real
Identities, and warily questioned every
Role. Under the sun's strobe, at my peril,
I staggered into an enamel sky,

Knowing my destiny would be geraniums,
Blood-red and quivering on a rickety wagon
I might never encounter, only watch them
Drop velvety petals as they rattled on.

HANDS

In a scary movie,
A severed hand crept a few inches,
Stopped, index finger in air,
And turned crab-like toward the audience.
That's when I got up from my velvety chair
In the matinee and moved two rows
Back, then three more when I peeked
Between my fingers and saw a hand
Moving toward us kids. I closed my eyes
When a girl – no, me! – screamed
As the organ moaned, a prelude
To the appearance of more severed parts?
I said nothing when I opened my eyes
And saw the hand on my knee.
I blinked. How did it crawl
From the screen and settle with a pinch
On my jeans? I looked up – a bald usher
Next to me, a finger in his mouth.
I jumped from that chair and hurried,
Shirttail out, for the lobby door.

Saturday, sometime in the early sixties,
Fear only cost a grubby dime.

242 GARY SOTO (1952–)

SINGLE, WATCHING FRED AND GINGER

If romance is a construct
then it should look more like work.
It's the quarter time half dips
before things get serious and full and fast.
It's RKO Deco, wedding caked and layered –
even Venice is too real for this.
For them. Fiction is beautiful, or maybe
that's backwards, I forget.
Some unknown extra's dress rises,
like a curtain to a dimensionless stage,
revealing dancers, and her legs, lovely.
For me, stuck in the cheap seats
of my own dream, with this
obstructed view, this luscious obstruction.

GEORGE YATCHISIN (1963–)   243

ACKNOWLEDGMENTS

Thanks are due to the following copyright holders for permission to reprint:

KIM ADDONIZIO: "Scary Movies" from *What is This Thing Called Love*, W.W. Norton & Company, 2004. Reprinted with permission from the poet. ELIZABETH ALEXANDER: "Early Cinema" from *Crave Radiance: New and Selected Poems 1990–2010*. Copyright © 2001 by Elizabeth Alexander. Reprinted with the permission of The Permissions Company, Inc. on behalf of Graywolf Press, Minneapolis, Minnesota, www.graywolfpress.org. Faith Childs Agency. MEENA ALEXANDER: "South Indian Cinema" copyright © Meena Alexander, 2018. All rights reserved. Reprinted with permission from the poet. JOHN ALLMAN: "Loew's Triboro" by John Allman, from *Loew's Triboro*, copyright © 2004 by John Allman. Reprinted by permission of New Directions Publishing Corp. DAVID BAKER: "Violence" from *The Truth About Small Towns*, University of Arkansas Press, 1998. Reprinted with permission of the author. ANGELA BALL: "To Lon Chaney in *The Unknown*" from *Talking Pillow*, University of Pittsburgh Press. Reprinted with permission from the poet. FRANK BIDART: "Poem Ending with a Sentence by Heath Ledger" from *Metaphysical Dog*, Farrar, Straus & Giroux, 2013. RICHARD BRAUTIGAN: "Mrs Myrtle Tate, Movie Projectionist" from *Rommel Drives On Deep into Egypt*. Copyright © 1989 by Richard Brautigan. Sarah Lazin Books. Permission from Ianthe Brautigan for the Brautigan Estate. KURT